STRUM & SING John Denver

ISBN 978-1-57560-675-0

Visit our website at
www.cherrylane.com

contents

All This Joy

Words and Music by
John Denver

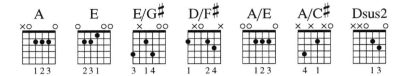

Verse 1

E |A | E/G♯|D/F♯ A/E |A
All this joy, all this   sor - row,

  A/C♯ |E |Dsus2 |A |
All this   promise,   all this pain.

E |A | E/G♯|D/F♯ A/E |A
Such is life, such is   be - ing,

  A/C♯ |E |Dsus2 |A |
Such is   spirit,   such is love.

Verse 2

E ||A | E/G♯|D/F♯ A/E |A
City of joy, city of   sor - row,

  A/C♯ |E |Dsus2 |A |
City of   promise,   city of pain.

E |A | E/G♯|D/F♯ A/E |A
Such is life, such is   be - ing,

  A/C♯ |E |Dsus2 |A |
Such is   spirit,   such is love.

Verse 3

```
       E        ‖A  |        E/G♯| D/F♯ A/E      |A
World of joy, world of    sor - row,

           A/C♯ |E           |Dsus2        |A       |
World of    promise,         world of pain.

       E       |A   |      E/G♯ |D/F♯ A/E     |A
Such is life, such is     be - ing,

           A/C♯ |E        |Dsus2        |A       |
Such is      spirit,       such is love.
```

Verse 4

```
       E        ‖A  |      E/G♯|D/F♯ A/E       |A
All this joy, all this    sor - row,

           A/C♯ |E            |Dsus2        |A       |
All this    promise,         all this pain.

       E      |A   |        E/G♯|D/F♯ A/E      |A
Such is life, such is     be - ing,

           A/C♯ |E        |Dsus2        |A       |
Such is      spirit,       such is love.

           A/C♯ |E        |Dsus2        |A       |       |       |       ‖
Such is      spirit,       such is love.
```

Annie's Song

Words and Music by
John Denver

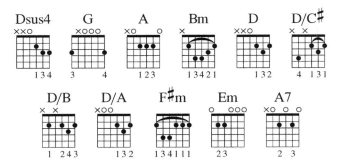

Verse 1

|Dsus4 ‖G |A |Bm
You fill up my sens - es

 |G |D |D/C♯ |D/B
Like a night in a forest,

 |D/A |G |F♯m |Em
Like the mountains in spring - time,

 |G |A7 | |
Like a walk in the rain.

 |A7 |G |A |Bm
Like a storm in the des - ert,

 |G |D |D/C♯ |D/B
Like a sleepy blue ocean,

 |D/A |G |F♯m |Em
You fill up my sens - es,

 |A7 |D |Dsus4 |D |
Come fill me a - gain.

Verse 2

Dsus4 ‖ **G** | **A** | **Bm**
Come let me love you,

| **G** | **D** | **D/C♯** | **D/B**
Let me give my life to you,

| **D/A** | **G** | **F♯**m | **Em**
Let me drown in your laugh - ter,

| **G** | **A7** | | |
Let me die in your arms.

| **A7** | **G** | **A** | **Bm**
Let me lay down be - side you,

| **G** | **D** | **D/C♯** | **D/B** |
Let me always be with you,

D/A | **G** | **F♯**m | **Em**
Come let me love you,

| **A7** | **D** | **Dsus4** | **D**
Come love me a - gain.

Repeat Verse 1

Back Home Again

Words and Music by
John Denver

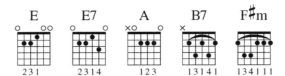

Verse 1

|E |E7 |A |
There's a storm across the valley, clouds are rollin' in,

|B7 | |E |
The afternoon is heavy on your shoul - ders.

|E |E7 |A |
There's a truck out on the four - lane a mile or more away,

|B7 | |E |
The whinin' of his wheels just makes it colder.

Verse 2

‖E |E7 |A |
He's an hour away from ridin' on your prayers up in the sky,

|B7 | |E |
And ten days on the road are barely gone.

|E |E7 |A |
There's a fire softly burning, supper's on the stove,

|B7 | |E | ‖
But it's the light in your eyes that makes him warm.

Chorus

A |B7 |E |E7 |A
Hey, it's good to be back home a-gain,

|B7 |E |A
Sometimes this old farm feels like a long-lost friend.

|B7 | |E
Yes 'n' hey, it's good to be back home again.

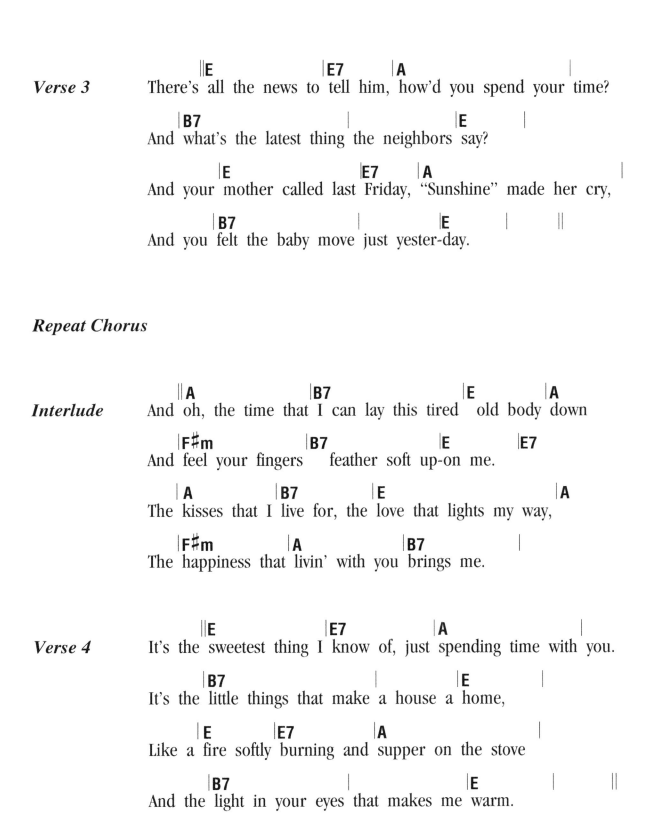

Verse 3

      ‖E |E7 |A

There's all the news to tell him, how'd you spend your time?

     |B7 | |E

And what's the latest thing the neighbors say?

        |E |E7 |A

And your mother called last Friday, "Sunshine" made her cry,

      |B7 | |E | ‖

And you felt the baby move just yester-day.

Repeat Chorus

Interlude

     ‖A |B7 |E |A

And oh, the time that I can lay this tired old body down

    |F♯m |B7 |E |E7

And feel your fingers feather soft up-on me.

    |A |B7 |E |A

The kisses that I live for, the love that lights my way,

    |F♯m |A |B7 |

The happiness that livin' with you brings me.

Verse 4

     ‖E |E7 |A |

It's the sweetest thing I know of, just spending time with you.

     |B7 | |E |

It's the little things that make a house a home,

    |E |E7 |A |

Like a fire softly burning and supper on the stove

     |B7 | |E | ‖

And the light in your eyes that makes me warm.

Repeat Chorus (2X)

Calypso

Words and Music by
John Denver

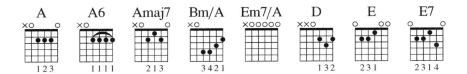

Verse 1

|A |A6
To sail on a dream on a crystal clear ocean,

|Amaj7 |A |Bm/A |
To ride on the crest of the wild raging storm,

|A |A6
To work in the service of life and the living,

|Amaj7   A | |Bm/A |
In search of the answers to questions un-known.

|A |A6 |
To be part of the movement and part of the growing,

Amaj7   A | |Em7/A | ||
Part of be-ginning to under-stand.

Chorus

D
Aye, Calypso,

|A
The places you've been to,

|D   A
The things that you've shown us,

|E   A |
The stories you tell.

D
Aye, Calypso,

|A
I sing to your spirit,

|D   A
The men who have served you

|E7   A |E |D A
So long and so well.

Verse 2

|| A | A6

Like the dolphin who guides you, you bring us beside you

| Amaj7 | A | Bm/A |

To light up the darkness and show us the way.

| A | A6

For though we are strangers in your silent world,

| Amaj7   A | | Bm/A |

To live on the land we must learn from the sea.

| A | A6 |

To be true as the tide and free as a wind-swell,

Amaj7   A | | Em7/A | ||

Joyful and loving in letting it be.

Repeat Chorus

Dancing with the Mountains

Words and Music by
John Denver

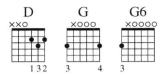

Verse 1

D
Everybody's got the dancin' fever,

D
Everybody loves to rock and roll.

D
Play it louder, baby, play it faster,

D
Funky music's gotta stretch your soul.

Verse 2

D
Just relax and let the rhythm take you,

D
Don't you be afraid to lose control.

D
If your heart has found some empty spaces,

D
Dancin's just a thing to make you whole.

Chorus 1

G | |D | |
I am one who dances with the moun-tains.

G | |D | |
I am one who dances in the wind.

G | |D |
I am one who dances on the o-cean.

|G |G6 |D | ‖
My partner's more than pieces, more than friends.

Verse 3

D | |
Were you there the night they lost the lightning?

D | |
Were you there the day the earth stood still?

D | |
Did you see the famous and the fighting?

D | ‖
Did you hear the prophet tell his tale?

Chorus 2

G | |D | |
We are one when dancing with the moun-tains.

G | |D | |
We are one when singing in the wind.

G | |D |
We are one when thinking of each oth-er,

|G |G6 |D | ‖
More than partners, more than pieces, more than friends.

Eagles and Horses
(I'm Flying Again)

Words and Music by
John Denver and Joe Henry

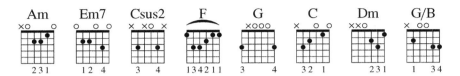

Verse 1

Am |Em7 |Am
Horses are creatures who worship the earth,

  |Am   Em7 |Csus2
They gallop on feet of ivo-ry.

  |F
Con-strained by the wonder of dying and birth,

  | Am   Em7 |Am G Am G |Am G Am G
The horses still run, they are free.

  |Am |Em7 |Am
My body is merely the shell of my soul,

  |Am   Em7 |Csus2
But the flesh must be given its due,

  |F
Like a pony that carries its rider back home,

  | Am   Em7 |Am G Am G |Am G Am G ||
Like an old friend who's tried and been true.

Chorus

C |G
I had a vision of eagles and horses

F   Dm |Am |G
High on a ridge in a race with the wind.

  |F |C G/B   Am
Going high - er and higher and fast-er and faster,

  |F   Am |C G |C | G/B |Am | | | ||
On eagles and horses I'm fly-ing a-gain.

Verse 2

|Am · · · |Em7 · · · |Am
Eagles inhabit the heavenly heights,

· · · · |Am · · · Em7 · · |Csus2
They know neither limit nor bound.

· · · · · · |F · · · · · · · | · · · · · · · |
They're the guardian angels of darkness and light,

· · · · |Am · · · · · Em7 · · |Am · G Am G |Am G Am G |
They see all and hear every sound.

· · · |Am · · · · · |Em7 · · · |Am
My spirit will never be broken or caught,

· · · · · |Am · · · Em7 · · |Csus2
For the soul is a free-flying thing,

· · · · · |F · · · · · · · | · · · · · · · |
Like an eagle that needs neither comfort nor thought

· · |Am · · · · Em7 · · |Am · G Am G |Am G Am G ||
To rise up on glorious wings.

Repeat Chorus

Verse 3

· · ||Am · · · · · |Em7 · · |Am
My body is merely the shell of my soul,

· · · · · |Am · · · Em7 · · |Csus2
But the flesh must be given its due,

· · · · · |F · · · · · · · | · · · · · · · |
Like a pony that carries its master back home,

· · · · |Am · · · · · Em7 · · · · |Am · G Am G |Am G Am G
Like an old friend who's tried and been true.

· · · |Am · · · · · |Em7 · · · |Am
My spirit will never be broken or caught,

· · · · · |Am · · · Em7 · · |Csus2
For the soul is a free-flying thing,

· · · · · |F · · · · · · · | · · · · · · · |
Like an eagle that needs neither comfort nor thought

· · |Am · · · · Em7 · · |Am · G Am G |Am G Am G ||
To rise up on glorious wings.

Repeat Chorus

Fly Away

Words and Music by
John Denver

Verse 1

G
All of her days have gone soft and cloudy,

G   **D7sus4**
All of her dreams have gone dry.

G
All of her nights have gone sad and shady,

G
She's getting ready to fly.

Chorus

Am |**D7**
Fly away,

Am |**D7**
Fly away,

      |**G**
Fly away.

Verse 2

G
Life in the city can make you crazy

 |**G** | **D7sus4**
For sounds of the sand and the sea.

G
Life in a high-rise can make you hungry

 |**G** |**D7sus4**
For things that you can't even see.

Repeat Chorus

Interlude

Am |**Bm** |**Cadd9** |
In this whole world there's nobod - y as lonely as she,

|**Am** |**D7** |**G** | | |
There's nowhere to go and there's no - where that she'd rather be.

Verse 3

‖**G** |
She's looking for lovers and children playing,

|**G** | **D7sus4**
She's looking for signs of the spring.

|**G** |
She listens for laughter and sounds of dancing,

|**G** |**D7sus4** ‖
She listens for any old thing.

Repeat Chorus

Repeat Interlude

Repeat Verse 1

Repeat Chorus

Follow Me

Words and Music by
John Denver

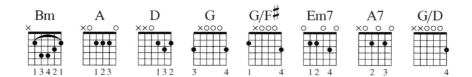

Bm   A   D   G   G/F#   Em7   A7   G/D

Intro

|Bm |A |D
It's by far the hardest thing I've ever done,

|G   G/F# |Em7 |A |A7
To be so in love with you and so a-lone.

Chorus

‖D |Em7 |D |G
Follow me   where I go,   what I do   and who I know,

|D |Em7 |A |A7
Make it part of you to be a part of me.

|D |Em7 |D |G |
Follow me   up and down,   all the way and all around,

D |G   A7 |D |
Take my hand and say you'll follow me.

Verse 1

‖D |A |G |D
It's long been on my mind, you know it's been a long, long time,

|Bm |A |G |A
I'll try to find the way that I can make you under-stand

|G |D |G |D
The way I feel about you and just how much I need you

|G   G/F# |Em7 G/D |G |A |A7
To be there where I   can talk to you when there's no one else around.

Repeat Chorus

Verse 2
 ‖**D** |**A** |**G** |**D** |
You see, I'd like to share my life with you and show you things I've seen,

Bm |**A** |**G** |**A**
Places that I'm going to, places where I've been

 |**G** |**D** |**G** |**D**
To have you there beside me and never be a-lone

 |**G** **G/F♯** |**Em7**   **G/D** |**G** |**A** |**A7**
And all the time that you're with me, then we will be at home.

Repeat Chorus

For Baby
(For Bobbie)

Words and Music by
John Denver

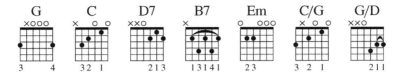

Verse 1

|G   C |G
I'll walk in the rain by your side,

|C   D7 |G
I'll cling to the warmth of your hand,

|C   D7 |G B7 Em
I'll do any-thing to help you un-der-stand,

|G   D7 |G
I'll love you more than anybody can.

Chorus 1

‖C   D7 |G |
And the wind will whisper your name to me,

C   D7 |G
Little birds will sing along in time,

|C   D7 |C/G
The leaves will bow down when you walk by,

|G C G/D D7 |G
And morn-ing bells will chime.

Verse 2

  ‖**G**   **C** |**G**
I'll be there when you're feeling down

  |**C**   **D7** |**G**
To kiss away the tears if you cry.

  |**C**   **D7** |**G** **B7** **Em**
I'll share with you all the happi-ness I've found,

  |**G**   **D7** |**G**
A re-flection of the love in your eyes.

Chorus 2

  ‖**C**   **D7** |**G**
And I'll sing you the songs of the rainbow,

  |**C**   **D7** |**G**
The whisper of the joy that is mine,

  |**C**   **D7** |**C/G**
The leaves will bow down when you walk by,

  |**G**   **C** **G/D** **D7** |**G**   ‖
And morn-ing bells will chime.

For You

Words and Music by
John Denver

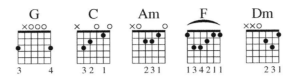

Verse 1

       G   **|C**   **|Am**
Just to look in your eyes again,

         |F   **|Dm**
Just to lay in your arms,

          |G   **|C**   **|G**
Just to be the first one always there for you.

         |C   **|Am**
Just to live in your laughter,

         |F   **|Dm**
Just to sing in your heart,

         |G   **|C**   **|**
Just to be every one of your dreams come true.

Verse 2

       G   **‖C**   **|Am**
Just to sit by your window,

         |F   **|Dm**
Just to touch in the night,

        |G   **|C**   **|G**
Just to offer a prayer each day for you.

         |C   **|Am**
Just to long for your kisses,

         |F   **|Dm**
Just to dream of your sighs,

         |G   **|C**   **|**
Just to know that I'd give my life for you.

STRUM & SING

Chorus 1

G ‖C |Am   F G
For you, all the rest   of my life.

|C |Am   F G
For you, all the best   of my life.

|C |G |C |
For you alone,   only for you.

Verse 3

G   ‖C |Am
Just to wake up each morning,

|F |Dm
Just to you by my side,

|G |C |G
Just to know that you're never really far a-way.

|C |Am
Just a reason for living,

|F |Dm
Just to say I a-dore,

|G |C |
Just to know that you're here in my heart to stay.

Chorus 2

G ‖C |Am   F G
For you, all the rest   of my life.

|C |Am   F G
For you, all the best   of my life.

|C |G |C   G ‖
For you alone,   only for you.

Outro

C |Am |F |Dm |G |C |G

|C |Am
Just the words of a love song,

|F |Dm
Just the beat of my heart,

|G |C | ‖
Just the pledge of my life, my love, for you.

Higher Ground

Words by John Denver and Joe Henry
Music by John Denver and Lee Holdridge

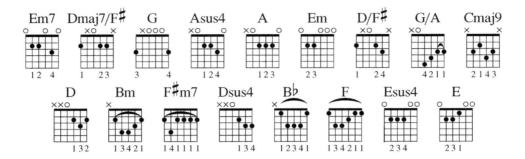

Verse 1

|Em7 |Dmaj7/F♯
There are those who can live

           |G |Asus4   A
With the things   they don't believe   in.

           |Em |D/F♯
They are giving up their lives

      |G |G/A   A |Cmaj9 |
For something that is less   than it can be.

Verse 2

       ||Em7 |Dmaj7/F♯
Some have longed for a home

  |G |Asus4   A
In a place of inspira - tion.

       |Em |D/F♯
Some will fill the emptiness   inside

 |G |G/A   A |Cmaj9 |
By giving it all for the things that they believe,

    |Asus4   A | ||
They be-lieve.

Chorus

A |D
Maybe it's just a dream in me,

Bm |F♯m7 |
Maybe it's just my style,

G |A |D Dsus4 D|
Maybe it's just the freedom that I've found.

   |A |D
But given the possibili-ty

   |Bm |G
Of living up to the dream in me,

   |Em7 |Asus4   A |D   Dsus4 D| |
You know that I'll be reach - ing for higher ground.

Verse 3

   ‖Em7 |Dmaj7/F♯
I will stand on my own,

   |G |Asus4   A
I will live up to this vi - sion.

   |Em |D/F♯
I will trust in what I feel

   |G |G/A   A |Cmaj9
And follow my heart un-til it brings me home,

   |Asus4   A | ‖
Brings me home.

Repeat Chorus

Interlude

B♭ |F |
Keep me through the night.

B♭ |F |
Lead me to the light.

G |D |
Teach me the magic of wonder.

G   Bm |Esus4 E | |Asus4 A | ‖
Give me the spir - it to fly.

Repeat Chorus (2X)

I'd Rather Be a Cowboy
(Lady's Chains)

Words and Music by
John Denver

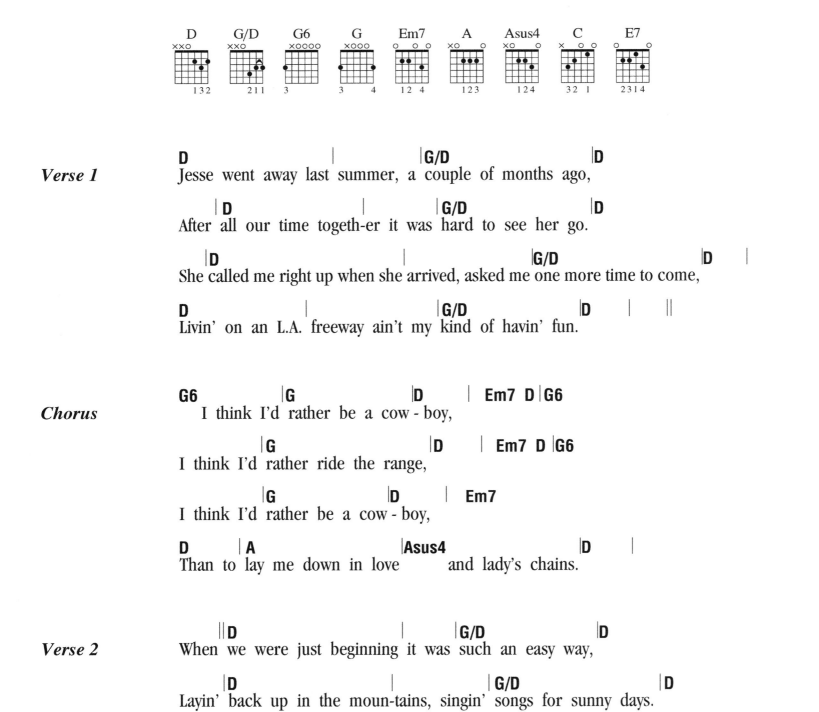

D   G/D   G6   G   Em7   A   Asus4   C   E7

Verse 1

D | | G/D | D
Jesse went away last summer, a couple of months ago,

| D | | G/D | D
After all our time togeth-er it was hard to see her go.

| D | | G/D | D |
She called me right up when she arrived, asked me one more time to come,

D | | G/D | D | | ||
Livin' on an L.A. freeway ain't my kind of havin' fun.

Chorus

G6 | G | D | Em7 D | G6
I think I'd rather be a cow-boy,

| G | D | Em7 D | G6
I think I'd rather ride the range,

| G | D | Em7
I think I'd rather be a cow-boy,

D | A | Asus4 | D |
Than to lay me down in love   and lady's chains.

Verse 2

|| D | | G/D | D
When we were just beginning it was such an easy way,

| D | | G/D | D
Layin' back up in the moun-tains, singin' songs for sunny days.

| D | | G/D | D
But she got tired of pickin' dai-sies and cookin' my meals for me,

| D | | G/D | D | ||
She can live the life she wants to, yes, and it's all right with me.

Repeat Chorus

Interlude

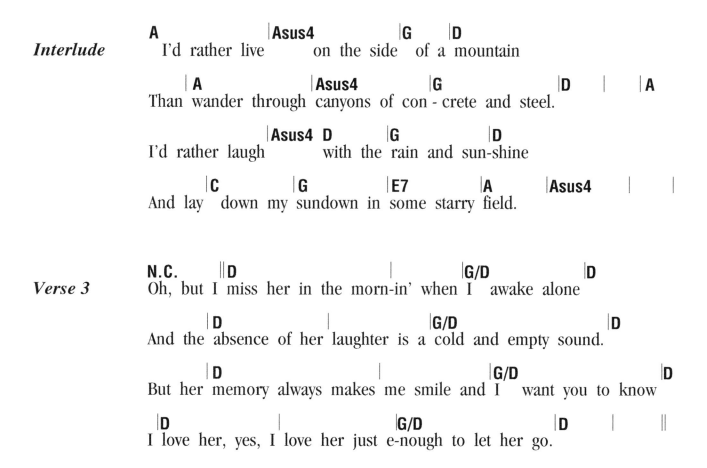

A | Asus4 | G | D
I'd rather live on the side of a mountain

| A | Asus4 | G | D | | A
Than wander through canyons of con - crete and steel.

| Asus4 D | G | D
I'd rather laugh with the rain and sun-shine

| C | G | E7 | A | Asus4 | |
And lay down my sundown in some starry field.

Verse 3

N.C. ‖D | | G/D | D
Oh, but I miss her in the morn-in' when I awake alone

| D | | G/D | D
And the absence of her laughter is a cold and empty sound.

| D | | G/D | D
But her memory always makes me smile and I want you to know

|D | | G/D | D | | ‖
I love her, yes, I love her just e-nough to let her go.

Repeat Chorus (2X)

It's About Time

Words and Music by
John Denver and Glen Hardin

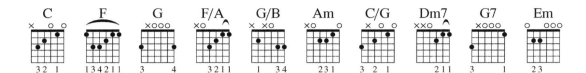

Verse 1

    |C |F |
There's a full moon over India and Gandhi lives again.

G   F/A   G/B |C   G
Who's to say   you have   to lose for someone else to win?

    |C |F
In the eyes of all the people the look is much the same,

    |G   F/A   G/B |C
For the first is just   the last   one when you play a deadly game.

Chorus 1

    ‖F   G |C
It's about time we realize it, we're all in this together.

   |F   G |C
It's about time we find out it's all of us or none.

    |F   G |C   G/B   Am
It's about time we recognize it, these changes in   the weather.

C/G |F   Dm7   G7 |C
It's about time, it's about changes and it's about time.

Verse 2

    ‖C |F
There's a light in the Vatican window for all the world to see,

   |G   F/A   G/B |C   G
And a voice cries in the wil - derness and some-times he speaks for me.

   |C |F
I sup-pose I love him most of all when he kneels to kiss the land,

   |G   G/B |C
With his lips upon our mother's breast he makes his strongest stand.

Chorus 2

‖**F**   **G** |**C**
It's about time we start to see it,   the earth is our only home.

|**F**   **G** |**C**
It's about time we start to face it,   we can't make it here all alone.

|**F**   **G** |**C**   **G/B**   **Am**
It's about time we start to lis-ten to the voices in   the wind.

C/G |**F**   **Dm7**   **G7** |**C** |**Am Em** |**F** |**C/G** |**G**
It's about time and it's about changes and it's about time.

Verse 3

‖**C** |**F**
There's a man who is my brother, I just don't know his name,

|**G**   **F/A**   **G/B** |**C**   **G**
But I know his home   and fam - ily because I know we feel the same.

|**C** |**F** |
And it hurts me when he's hungry and when his children cry.

G |**C**
I too am a father and that little one is mine.

Chorus 3

‖**F**   **G** |**C**
It's about time we begin it,   to turn the world around.

|**F**   **G** |**C**
It's about time we start to make it,   the dream we've always known.

|**F**   **G** |**C**   **G/B**   **Am**
It's about time we start to live it,   the family   of man.

C/G |**F**   **Dm7**   **G7** |**C**
It's about time, it's about changes and it's about time.

|**F**   **G**   **G7** |**C**
It's about peace and it's about plenty and it's about time.

|**F**   **G**   **G7** |**C**   ‖
It's about you and me to-gether and it's about time.

Leaving on a Jet Plane

Words and Music by
John Denver

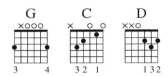

Verse 1

|G |C
All my bags are packed, I'm ready to go,

|G |C
I'm standing here out-side your door,

|G |C |D |
I hate to wake you up to say good-bye.

      |G |C
But the dawn is breakin', it's early morn,

     |G |C
The taxi's waitin', he's blowin' his horn,

  |G |C |D |
Al-ready I'm so lonesome I could die.

Chorus

‖G |C |
So kiss me and smile for me,

G |C |
Tell me that you'll wait for me,

G |C |D |
Hold me like you'll never let me go.

     |G |C |G
'Cause I'm leavin' on a jet plane,

      |C |G
Don't know when I'll be back again.

   |C |D | | |
Oh, babe, I hate to go.

Verse 2

‖G |C
There's so many times I've let you down,

|G |C
So many times I've played around,

|G |C |D |
I tell you now they don't mean a thing.

|G |C
Every place I go I'll think of you,

|G |C
Every song I sing I'll sing for you,

|G |C |D |
When I come back I'll bring your wedding ring.

Repeat Chorus

Verse 3

G |C |
Now the time has come to leave you,

G |C
One more time let me kiss you,

|G |C |D | |
Then close your eyes, I'll be on my way.

G |C
Dream about the days to come

|G |C
When I won't have to leave alone,

|G |C |D | ‖
A-bout the times I won't have to say:

Repeat Chorus

Outro

|G |C |G
I'm leavin' on a jet plane,

|C |G
Don't know when I'll be back again,

|C | |D | | | | |G   ‖
Oh, babe, I hate to go.

Love Again

Words and Music by
John Denver

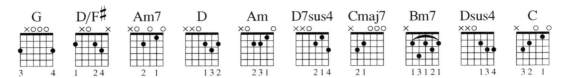

Verse 1

    G   **D/F♯**   **|Am7**
I didn't think   it could hap - pen again,

   |D   **Am**   **|G**   **|**
I'm just too old and set in my ways.

            D/F♯   **|Am7**   **D**   **|**
I was convinced   I would al - ways be lonely

Am   **D7sus4**   **|G**   **|**
All of the rest   of my days.

Cmaj7   **|Bm7**
Maybe I gave up on ro-mance

   |Am   **Am7**   **|Dsus4** **D**
In my longing to give up the pain,

   |G   **D/F♯**   **|Am7**   **D**   **|G Bm7 |C D ||**
I just didn't believe   I would ev - er love again.

Verse 2

    G   **D/F♯**   **|Am7**
I was like one   who had shut   myself in,

   |D   **Am**   **|G**
Closed the windows, locked all the doors,

  |G   **D/F♯**   **|Am7**   **D**
A-fraid of the dark   and the beat   of my heart,

   |Am   **D7sus4**   **|G**
And yet knowing there had   to be more.

   |Cmaj7   **|Bm7**
Though it sounds like a great contradic-tion,

  |Am7   **|Dsus4** **D**
It's the easiest thing to ex-plain:

   |G   **D/F♯**   **|Am** **D** **|G Bm7 |C D ||**
You see, I was afraid   I might never love a-gain.

Verse 3

G   D/F♯ |Am7
What does it take   for a blind   man to see

                    |D   Am |G |
That there's more there than just meets the eye?

G   D/F♯ |Am7   D
What are the ways   that the mag - ic comes in

          |Am   D7sus4 |G |
That can turn a song in   -   to a sigh?

Cmaj7 |Bm7
Sometimes I think that I'm dream-ing,

    |Am7 |Dsus4   D
Or maybe I'm going in-sane,

    |G   D/F♯ |Am   D |G Bm7 |C D ||
Or maybe it's just   that I'm falling in love again.

Outro

Cmaj7 |Bm7
Here I am standing be-side you.

    |Am7 |Dsus4 D |
Ah, life's such a wonderful game!

G   D/F♯ |Am   D |G   D/F♯|Am D |
Look at me now,   I've fallen in love a-gain.

G   D/F♯ |Am   D |G Bm7 |C D |G ||
Look at me now,   I've fallen in love again!

My Sweet Lady

Words and Music by
John Denver

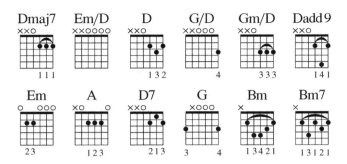

Verse 1

Dmaj7 |Em/D
Lady, are you crying?

     |D   Dmaj7 |G/D Gm/D
Do the tears be-long to me?

     |D   Dmaj7 |Dadd9 Dmaj7 |Em |A |
Did you think our time to-gether   was all gone?

Dmaj7 |Em/D
Lady, you've been dreaming,

     |D   Dmaj7 |G/D Gm/D
I'm as close as I   can be

     |Dmaj7 |Em   A |D |D7 ||
And I swear to you our time has just be-gun.

Chorus

G |A |D |D7
Close your eyes and rest your weary mind,

|G |A |D |D7
I promise I will stay right here be-side you.

|G |A |D |
To-day our lives were joined, became en-twined,

|Bm |Bm7 |Em |A ||
I wish that you could know how much I love you.

Verse 2

Dmaj7 |Em/D

Lady, are you happy?

        |D   Dmaj7 |G/D Gm/D

Do you feel the way I do?

      |D   Dmaj7 |Dadd9 Dmaj7   Em |A

Are there meanings that you've never   seen be-fore?

Dmaj7 |Em/D

Lady, my sweet lady,

    |D   Dmaj7 |G/D Gm/D

I just can't be-lieve it's true,

      |Dmaj7 |Em A |D |D7 ||

And it's like I've never ever loved be-fore.

Repeat Chorus

Verse 3

Dmaj7 |Em/D

Lady, are you crying?

     |D   Dmaj7 |G/D Gm/D

Do the tears be-long to me?

    |D   Dmaj7 |Dadd9 Dmaj7 |Em |A

Did you think our time to-gether   was all gone?

Dmaj7 |Em/D

Lady, my sweet lady,

  |D   Dmaj7 |G/D Gm/D

I'm as close as I   can be

     |Dmaj7 |Em   A |D | ||

And I swear to you our time has just be-gun.

Never a Doubt

Words and Music by
John Denver

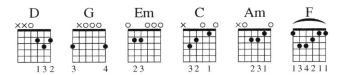

Verse 1

     D |G   Em
I suppose there have been times

          |C   D |G   Em
When you felt like a room full of dark - ness,

     |C   D
Not a win - dow around.

   |G   Em |C   D |G Em |C
There must have been mo - ments you felt you were truly alone.

D |G   Em |C D |G Em
Then again each of us knows, in a night of un-bearable sad - ness

      |C   D
Still a light can be found,

   |G   Em |C   D |G Em |C
In each morning the prom - ise that someday your true love will come.

Chorus

     D ||G   Em |C   D |G Em
There was never a doubt, never a doubt in my mind

       |C   D |
We weren't meant to be lone - ly,

G   Em |C   D |G Em |C
Never a doubt I knew that I'd find you someday.

     D |G   Em |C   D |G Em
There was never a doubt, after all of those nights all alone,

      |C   D |
All those des - perate morn - ings,

G   Em |C   D |G   Em |C
Never a doubt, there was never a doubt in my mind.

Verse 2

D ‖G   Em
I suppose there are some peo - ple

    |C   D |G Em
Who nev - er believe in the mag - ic,

    |C   D
Oh, the mag - ic of love.

  |G   Em |C   D |G Em |C
They think nothing is pre - cious and life is just pleasure and pain.

D |G   Em |C   D |G Em
Then again each of us knows, when a heart has been broken it's trag - ic.

    |C   D
Oh, the mag - ic of love.

  |G   Em |C   D |G Em |C
Even that which is bro - ken with love can be mended again.

Interlude

‖Am |F
 All the things that you fear, at the most,

   |C | |Am
They mean nothing,

    |F |G |
All the sorrow and sadness can just disappear.

Outro-Chorus

F G ‖C   Am |F   G |C Am
There was never a doubt, never a doubt in my mind

     |F   G |
We weren't meant to be lone - ly,

C   Am |F   G |C Am |F
Never a doubt I knew that I'd find you someday.

  G |C   Am |F   G |C Am
There was never a doubt, after all of those nights all a-lone,

    |F   G |
All those des - perate morn - ings,

C   Am |F   G |C Am
Never a doubt, there was never a doubt in my mind.

  |F   G |C Am
There was never a doubt in my mind.

  |F   G |C Am |F G |C ‖
There was never a doubt in my mind.

Perhaps Love

Words and Music by
John Denver

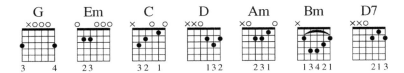

Verse 1

|G   Em
Perhaps love is like a resting place,

|C   D
A shelter from the storm.

|G   Em
It ex-ists to give you com - fort,

|Am   D
It is there to keep you warm.

|Bm   Em
And in those times of trou - ble

|C   D
When you are most alone,

|Am   D |G   D7
The memory of love will bring you home.

Verse 2

‖G   Em
Perhaps love is like a win-dow,

|C   D
Per-haps an open door.

|G   Em
It in-vites you to come clos - er,

|Am   D
It wants to show you more.

|Bm   Em
And even if you lose yourself

|C   D
And don't know what to do,

|Am   D |G
The memory of love will see you through.

Interlude

‖**Bm**   **Em**
Oh, love to some is like a cloud,

|**C**   **D** **G**
To some as strong as steel,

|**Bm**   **Em**
For some a way of living,

|**C**   **D** **G**
For some a way to feel.

|**Bm**   **Em**
And some say love is holding on,

|**C**   **D**   **G**
And some say letting go,

|**Bm**   **Em**
And some say love is everything,

|**Am**   **D** |
And some say they don't know.

Verse 3

‖**G**   **Em**
Perhaps love is like the o-cean,

|**C**   **D**
Full of conflict, full of change,

|**G**   **Em**
Like a fire when it's cold   outside

|**Am**   **D**
Or thunder when it rains.

|**Bm**   **Em**
If I   should live for-ever

|**C**   **D**
And all my dreams come true,

|**Am**   **D** |**G**   ‖
My memories of love will be of you.

Poems, Prayers and Promises

Words and Music by
John Denver

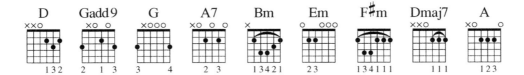

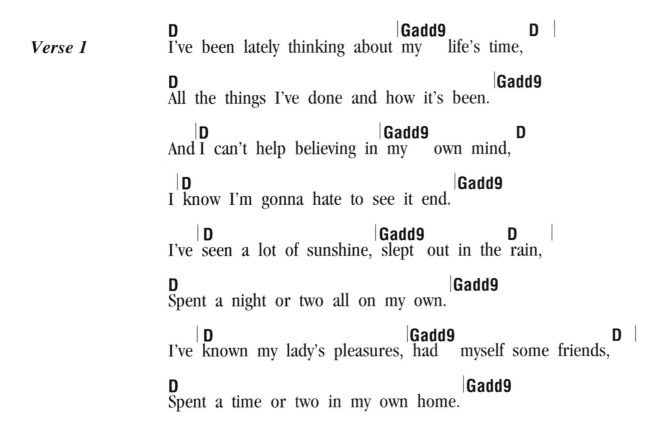

Verse 1

D |**Gadd9**   **D** |
I've been lately thinking about my life's time,

D |**Gadd9**
All the things I've done and how it's been.

 |**D** |**Gadd9**   **D**
And I can't help believing in my own mind,

 |**D** |**Gadd9**
I know I'm gonna hate to see it end.

 |**D** |**Gadd9**   **D** |
I've seen a lot of sunshine, slept out in the rain,

D |**Gadd9**
Spent a night or two all on my own.

 |**D** |**Gadd9**   **D** |
I've known my lady's pleasures, had myself some friends,

D |**Gadd9**
Spent a time or two in my own home.

Chorus

‖**G**   **A7**   **|D**   **G**
I have to say it now, it's been a good life all in all.

            |D   **Bm**   **|Em A7**
It's really fine to have a chance to hang around

    |G   **A7** **|D**   **G**
And lie there by the fire and watch the evening tire,

         |D   **Bm**   **|Em**   **A7**
While all my friends and my old la - dy sit and pass a pipe around,

        |G   **F♯m**   **|G**   **D**
And talk of poems and prayers and promises and things that we be-lieve in.

    |D   **Dmaj7**   **|G**   **A**
How sweet it is to love someone, how right it is to care.

    |G   **F♯m**   **|Em**   **D**
How long it's been since yes - terday, what about to-morrow

    |D   **Dmaj7**   **|G**   **A**   **|**   **|D**   **| G D**
And what about our dreams and all the memories we share?

Verse 2

    ‖**D**   **|Gadd9**   **D**   **|**
The days they pass so quickly now, the nights are seldom long.

D   **|Gadd9**
Time around me whispers when it's cold.

    |D   **|Gadd9**   **D**
The changes somehow frighten me, still I have to smile.

    |D   **|Gadd9**
It turns me on to think of growing old.

    |D   **|Gadd9**   **D**
For though my life's been good to me, there's still so much to do,

    |D   **|Gadd9**
So many things my mind has never known.

    |D   **|Gadd9**   **D**
I'd like to raise a family, I'd like to sail away

    |D   **|Gadd9**
And dance across the mountains on the moon.

Repeat Chorus

Prisoners
(Hard Life, Hard Times)

Words and Music by
John Denver

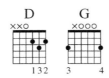

Verse 1

  D
Josie works a counter at the down-town five and dime,

   G   **D**
Anything   at all to help her pass the time.

   D
Her mama keeps the baby and grandpa rambles on

     G   **D**
About the good times a playin' in his mind.

Chorus 1

    G   **D**
It's a hard   life livin' when you're lone - ly,

    G   **D**
It's a long   night sleepin' alone,

    G   **D**
It's a hard   time waiting for tomor - row,

    G   **D** | **G** **D**
It's a long,   long way home.

Verse 2

  D
Josie spends the evening with the peo-ple on the pages

     G   **D**
Of the pa - perback she picked up at the store.

   D
Well, sometimes it's the TV, she'll try to write a letter,

G   **D**
They don't come too often anymore.

STRUM & SING

Chorus 2

‖**G** |**D**
It's a hard life livin' when you're lone - ly,

|**G** |**D**
It's a long night sleepin' alone,

|**G** |**D**
It's a hard time waiting for tomor - row,

|**G** |**D** | | |**G**
It's a long, long way home.

Interlude

‖**D** |**G** |
I stare at the gray walls before me,

D |**G**
I see her face in the dawn.

|**D** |**G**
I try to imagine our ba - by,

|**D** |**G**
I wish they would let me go home,

|**D** |**G** |**D**
I wish they would let me go home.

Outro-Chorus

‖**G** |**D**
It's a hard life livin' when you're lone - ly,

|**G** |**D**
It's a long night sleepin' alone,

|**G** |**D**
It's a hard time waiting for tomor - row,

|**G** |**D**
It's a long, long way home.

|**G** |**D**
It's a long, long way home.

|**G** |**D**
Bring me and the other boys home,

|**G** |**D** | ‖
Bring me and the other boys home.

Rhymes and Reasons

Words and Music by
John Denver

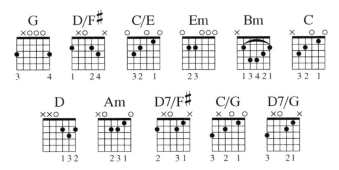

Verse 1

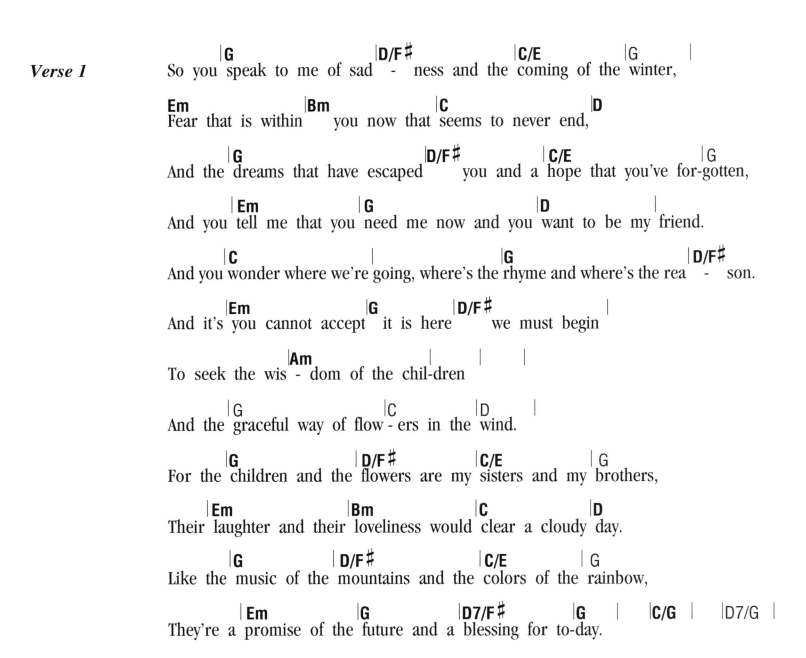

|G |D/F# |C/E |G |
So you speak to me of sad - ness and the coming of the winter,

Em |Bm |C |D
Fear that is within   you now that seems to never end,

|G |D/F# |C/E |G
And the dreams that have escaped   you and a hope that you've for-gotten,

|Em |G |D |
And you tell me that you need me now and you want to be my friend.

|C | |G |D/F#
And you wonder where we're going, where's the rhyme and where's the rea - son.

|Em |G |D/F# |
And it's you cannot accept   it is here   we must begin

|Am | | |
To seek the wis - dom of the chil-dren

|G |C |D |
And the graceful way of flow - ers in the wind.

|G |D/F# |C/E |G
For the children and the flowers are my sisters and my brothers,

|Em |Bm |C |D
Their laughter and their loveliness would clear a cloudy day.

|G |D/F# |C/E |G
Like the music of the mountains and the colors of the rainbow,

|Em |G |D7/F# |G |C/G |D7/G |
They're a promise of the future and a blessing for to-day.

Verse 2

        ‖ **G**   **|D/F♯**   **|C/E**   **|** G
Though the cities start to crum - ble and the towers fall a-round us,

    |Em   **|Bm**   **|C**   **|D**
The sun is slowly fad - ing and it's colder than the sea.

     |G   **|D/F♯**   **|C/E**   **|**G
It is written: From the des - ert to the mountains they shall lead us

    |Em   **|G**   **|D**   **|**
By the hand and by the heart and they will comfort you and me

     |C   **|**   **|G**   **|D/F♯** **|**
In their innocence and trusting, they will teach us to be free.

Em   **|G**   **|D/F♯**   **|**   **|Am**   **|**   **|**   **|G**   **|C**   **|D**   **|**

    |G   **|D/F♯**   **|C/E**   **|G**
For the children and the flowers are my sisters and my brothers,

    |Em   **|Bm**   **|C**   **|D**
Their laughter and their loveliness would clear a cloudy day.

    |G   **|D/F♯**   **|C/E**   **|G**   **|**
And the song that I am singing is a prayer to nonbe-lievers.

Em   **|G**   **|D7/F♯**   **|C/G**   **|**   **|**
Come and stand be-side us, we can find a better way.

G   **|**   **|C/G**   **|**   **|D7/G**   **|**   **|G**   ‖

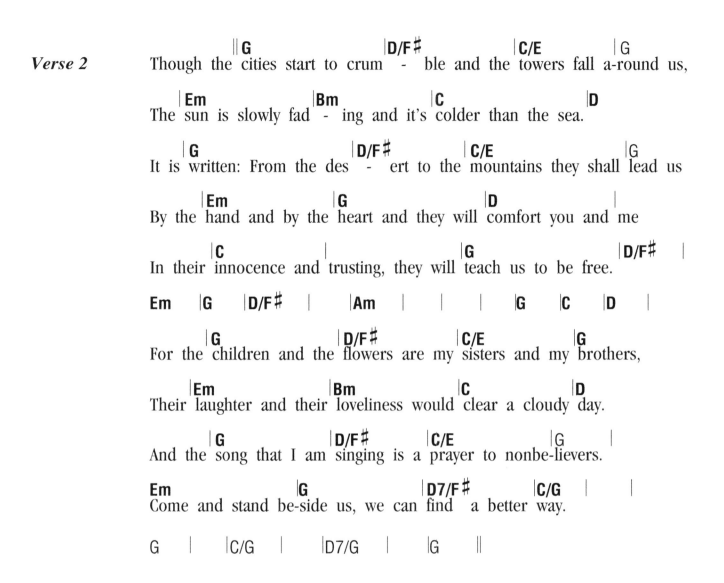

Seasons of the Heart

Words and Music by
John Denver

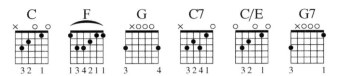

Verse 1

|C |F
Of course we have our differences, you shouldn't be surprised,

|G |C
It's as natural as changes in the seasons and the skies.

|C |F
Some-times we grow together, some-times we drift apart.

|G |C
A wiser man than I might know the seasons of the heart.

|C |F
And I'm walking here beside you in the early evening chill,

|G |C
A thing we've always loved to do, I know we always will.

|C |F
We have so much in common, so many things we share,

|G |C |C7 ||
That I can't believe my heart when it im-plies that you're not there.

Chorus 1

F   G |C |
Love is why I came here in the first place,

F   G |C   C/E |
Love is now the reason I must go.

F   G |C |
Love is all I ever hoped to find here,

F   G |C |F |C |G7
Love is still the only dream I know.

Verse 2

‖C |F
And so I don't know how to tell you, it's difficult to say,

|G |C
I never in my wildest dreams i-magined it this way.

|C   C/E |F
Some-times I just don't know you, there's a stranger in our home.

|G |C
When I'm lying right beside you is when I'm most alone.

|C |F
And I think my heart is broken, there's an emptiness inside.

|G |C
So many things I've longed for have so often been denied.

|C   C/E |F
Still I, I wouldn't try to change you, there's no one that's to blame,

|G |C |C7   ‖
It's just some things that mean so much, we just don't feel the same.

Chorus 2

F   G |C |
Love is why I came here in the first place,

F   G |C   C/E |
Love is now the reason I must go.

F   G |C |
Love is all I ever hoped to find here,

F   G |C
Love is still the only dream I know.

|F |G |C |F |C | ‖
True love is still the only dream I know.

A Song for All Lovers

Words and Music by
John Denver

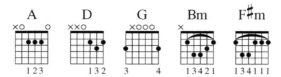

Chorus

|**A** | | | |**D** | |
I see them dancing   some-where in the moonlight,

|**D** |**A** | | | |**D** | | |
Somewhere in Alas - ka,   some-where in the sun.

D |**A** | | | |**D** | |
I hear them sing - ing   a song for all lovers,

|**D** |**A** | | | |**D** | |
A song for the two hearts beating only as one.

Verse 1

|**D** ||**A** | | |**D** | |
I-magine the morn - ing,   no long-er a-lone,

|**D** |**A** | | | |**D** | |
The arms of an-other,   a place to belong.

|**D** |**G** |**A** | |**D** | |
No longer the strug - gle,   no longer the night,

|**D** |**A** | | | |**D** | |
And ever becom - ing   in the quickening light.

Verse 2

|D ‖A | | |D | |
To see in the dark - ness,   to lis-ten with-in,

|D |A | | |D | |
To answer in kindness,   to ever begin.

|D |G | |A |D | |
To ever be gen - tle,   to always be strong,

|D |A | | |D | |
To walk in the won - der,   to live in the song.

Interlude

|D ‖Bm | |G |A |D | |
In a place of enchant - ment   where the wild things are known.

|D |F♯m | |A |D | |
Will the future remem - ber   when the lovers are gone?

|D |G | |A |D | |
To ever be gen - tle,   to always be strong,

|D |A | | |D | | |
To walk in the won - der,   to live in the song.

Repeat Chorus

Outro

|D |A | |
A song for the two hearts

|A |D | | | | | | ‖
Beating only as one.

Sunshine on My Shoulders

Words by John Denver
Music by John Denver, Mike Taylor and Dick Kniss

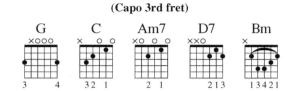

Chorus

G   C |G   C |G   C G C |
Sunshine on my shoulders makes me happy,

G   C |G   C |Am7 |D7 |
Sunshine in my eyes can make me cry.

G   C |G   C |G   C G C |
Sunshine on the water looks so lovely,

G   C |G   C |G C G C ||
Sunshine almost always makes me high.

Verse 1

G Am7 |Bm C |G   Am7 |Bm C
If I had a day that I could give you,

|G   Am7 |Bm C |Am7 |D7 |
I'd give to you   a day just like to-day.

G Am7 |Bm C |G   Am7 |Bm C
If I had   a song that I could sing for you,

|G   Am7 |Bm   C |G Am7 |Bm C ||
I'd sing a song   to make you feel this way.

Repeat Chorus

Verse 2
G   Am7 |Bm C |G   Am7 |Bm C
If I had a tale that I could tell you,

|G   Am7 |Bm C |Am7 |D7 |
I'd tell a tale   sure to make you smile.

G   Am7 |Bm C |G   Am7 |Bm C
If I had   a wish that I could wish for you,

|G   Am7 |Bm   C |G Am7 |Bm C ||
I'd make a wish   for sunshine all the while.

Repeat Chorus

Outro
G   C |G   C |G Am7 |Bm C |
Sunshine almost all the time makes me high.

G   C |G   C |G Am7 |Bm C G ||
Sunshine almost always…

Take Me Home, Country Roads

Words and Music by
John Denver, Bill Danoff and Taffy Nivert

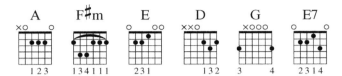

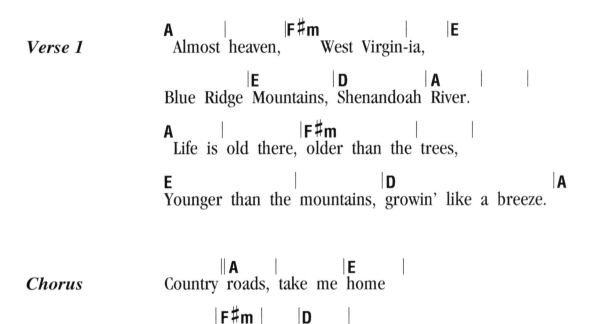

Verse 1

A | **F#m** | **E**
Almost heaven,   West Virgin-ia,

E | **D** | **A** | |
Blue Ridge Mountains, Shenandoah River.

A | **F#m** | |
Life is old there, older than the trees,

E | **D** | **A**
Younger than the mountains, growin' like a breeze.

Chorus

‖ **A** | **E** |
Country roads, take me home

| **F#m** | **D** |
To the place I be-long:

| **A** | **E** |
West Vir-ginia, mountain momma,

| **D** | **A** | ‖
Take me home, country roads.

Verse 2

A | |F♯m | |E
All my memories   gather 'round her,

|E |D |A | |
Miner's lady, stranger to blue water.

A | |F♯m | |
Dark and dusty, painted on the sky,

E | |D |A
Misty taste of moonshine, teardrop in my eye.

Repeat Chorus

Interlude

F♯m |E |A |
I hear her voice, in the mornin' hour she calls me,

|D |A |E |
The radio re-minds me of my home far a-way,

|F♯m |G |D
And drivin' down the road I get a feelin'

|A |E |E7 |
That I should have been home yesterday, yester-day.

Outro-Chorus

‖A | |E |
Country roads, take me home

|F♯m | |D |
To the place I be-long:

|A | |E |
West Vir-ginia, mountain momma,

|D | |A |
Take me home, country roads.

|E | |A |
Take me home, country roads,

|E | |A | ‖
Take me home, country roads.

This Old Guitar

Words and Music by
John Denver

(Capo 2nd fret)

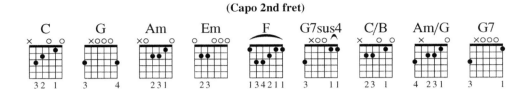

Verse 1

     C |G |Am |Em |F
This old guitar taught me to sing   a love   song,

                   |G7sus4 |C C/B |Am Am/G
It showed me how to laugh   and how to cry.

        |F |G |C   C/B |Am Am/G
It intro-duced me to some friends   of mine and brightened up some days

       |F |G7sus4 |C   C/B |Am Am/G
And it helped me make it through   some lonely nights.

       |F |G7 |C C/B |Am Am/G |F |G7sus4 G7 ||
What a friend to have on a cold and lonely night.

Verse 2

     C |G |Am |Em
This old guitar gave me my love - ly la - dy,

   |F |G7sus4 |C   C/B |Am Am/G
It opened up her eyes   and ears to me.

   |F |G |C   C/B |Am Am/G
It brought us close togeth-er and I guess it broke her heart,

   |F |G |C C/B |Am Am/G
It opened up the space for us to be.

   |F |G7sus4   G7 |C C/B |Am Am/G |F |G7sus4 G7 ||
What a lovely place and a lovely space   to be.

Verse 3

C |G |Am |Em |
This old guitar   gave me my life,   my liv - ing,

F |G7sus4 |C   C/B |Am Am/G
All the things you know   I love to do,

 |F |G |C   C/B |Am Am/G
To serenade the stars that shine from a sunny mountainside

 |F |G |C C/B |Am Am/G |F
And most of all to sing   my songs for you.

 |G7sus4   G7 |C
I love to sing   my songs   for you.

Outro

C/B   ‖Am   Am/G |F
Yes, I do,   you know,

                        |G7 |C   C/B |Am Am/G |F |G7sus4 G7 |C   ‖
And I love to sing   my songs for you.

Whispering Jesse

Words and Music by
John Denver

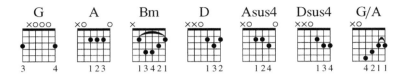

Verse 1

|G A |Bm G |D |G
I often have wan-dered   in deep contempla - tion,

A |Bm A |G |Asus4 |A
It seems that the mind runs wild when you're all a-lone.

G |D |G
The way that it could be,

A |D |G
The way that it should be,

A |Bm A |G A |D |
Things I'd do dif - f'rent-ly if I could do them a-gain.

Verse 2

||G A |Bm G |D |G
I've always loved spring-time,   the passing of win - ter,

A |Bm A |G |Asus4 |A
The green of the new leaves and life goin' on.

G |D |G
The promise of morning,

A |D |G
The long days of summer,

A |Bm A |G A |D |
Warm nights of lov - ing her be-neath the bright stars.

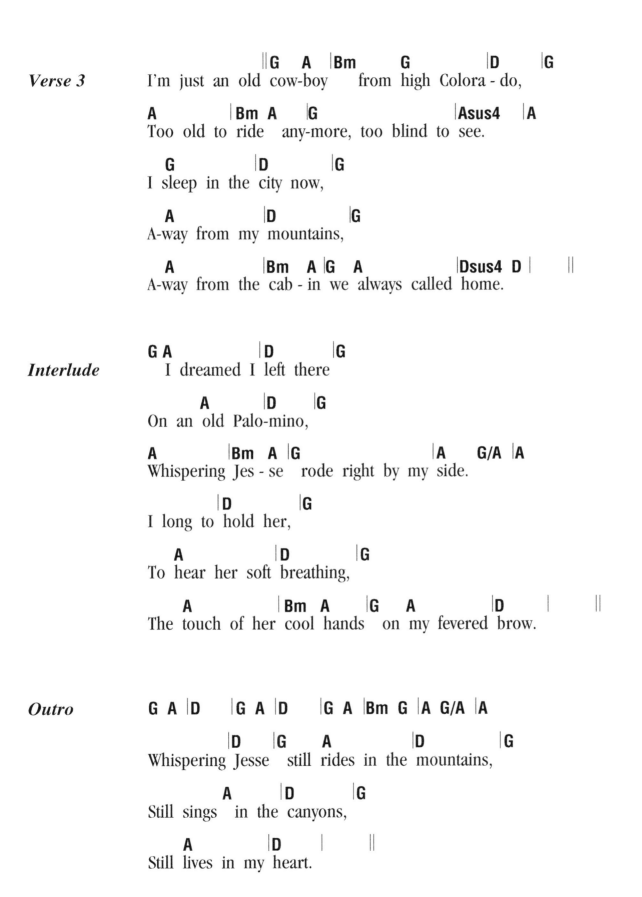

Verse 3

```
         ‖G  A  |Bm      G          |D      |G
I'm just an old cow-boy     from high Colora - do,

A        |Bm A  |G              |Asus4  |A
Too old to ride  any-more, too blind to see.

  G          |D      |G
I sleep in the city now,

  A          |D      |G
A-way from my mountains,

  A          |Bm  A |G  A          |Dsus4 D |       ‖
A-way from the cab - in we always called home.
```

Interlude

```
G A          |D      |G
  I dreamed I left there

    A        |D      |G
On an old Palo-mino,

A        |Bm  A |G              |A    G/A |A
Whispering Jes - se  rode right by my side.

       |D      |G
I long to hold her,

  A          |D      |G
To hear her soft breathing,

  A          |Bm  A  |G  A       |D    |       ‖
The touch of her cool hands  on my fevered brow.
```

Outro

```
G  A |D  |G  A  D  |G  A |Bm  G |A  G/A |A

         |D  |G      A          |D      |G
Whispering Jesse  still rides in the mountains,

          A        |D      |G
Still sings  in the canyons,

  A          |D    |       ‖
Still lives in my heart.
```

Windsong

Words and Music by
John Denver and Joe Henry

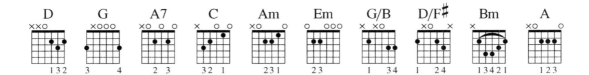

Verse 1

|D
The wind is the whisper of our mother the earth,

|D |G
The wind is the hand of our father the sky.

|G
The wind watches over our struggles and pleasures,

|G |D |A7
The wind is the goddess who first learned to fly.

Verse 2

‖D
The wind is the bearer of bad and good tidings,

|D |G
The weaver of darkness, the bringer of dawn.

|G
The wind gives the rain, then builds us a rainbow,

|G |C
The wind is the singer who sang the first song.

Interlude

```
 ‖Am                        |D
The wind is a twister of    anger and warning,

    |G              Em          |C              Am
The wind brings the fragrance of freshly mown hay.

    |C                      |D
The wind is a racer and a white stallion running,

         |C    G/B    Am  G   |D/F♯  Bm      |A      |A7
And the sweet taste of love on a slow  summer's day.
```

Verse 3

```
     ‖D                                 |
The wind knows the songs of the cities and canyons,

     |D                        |           |G
The thunder of mountains, the roar of the sea.

     |G                        |
The wind is the taker and giver of mornings,

     |G                        |           |D    |A7
The wind is the symbol of all that is free.
```

Verse 4

```
     ‖D                        |                |
So welcome the wind and the wisdom she offers,

 D                         |           |G
Follow her summons when she calls a-gain.

         |G                        |                |
In your heart and your spirit let the breezes surround you,

 G                         |           |C
Lift up your voice then and sing with the wind.
```

Outro

```
     |Am                      |D                |
La, la, la, la, la, la, la, la, la, la, la, la, la, la.

 C    G/B           Am  G          |D/F♯ Bm |A      |A7      |D       ‖
Dee, dee, dee, dee,     dee, dee, dee,      ooo.
```

Amazon
(Let This Be a Voice)

Words and Music by
John Denver

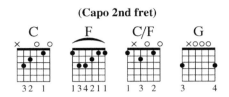

(Capo 2nd fret)

Verse 1

             |C |F |C | |
There is a river that runs from the mountains.

C |F |C | |
That one river is all rivers.

F C/F F| C/F   F |C |
All   rivers   are that one.

Verse 2

             ||C |F |C | |
There is a tree that stands in the forest.

C |F |C | |
That one tree is all forests.

F C/F F| C/F   F |C |
All   trees   are that one.

Verse 3

             ||C |F |C | |
There is a flower that blooms in the desert.

C |F |C | |
That one blossom is all flowers.

F C/F F| C/F   F |C |
All   flowers   are that one.

Verse 4

```
          ‖C           |F           |C           |           |
There  is  a  bird  that  sings  in  the  jungle.

C                       |F   |C           |           |
That  one  song  is  all   music.

F  C/F  F |      C/F    F        |C        |        ‖
All         songs    are  that  one.
```

Chorus 1

```
F        G           |C           |
It  is  the  song  of  life.

F        G               |C           |
It  is  the  flower  of  faith.

F        G               |C           |
It  is  the  tree  of  tempta - tion.

F        G           |C  G  C   |  G  C
It  is  the  river  of  no    re-grets.
```

Verse 5

```
          ‖C           |F           |C           |           |
There  is  a  child  that  cries  in  the  ghetto.

C                   |F           |C           |           |
That  one  child  is  all  of  our  children.

F   C/F  F   |        C/F    F        |C           |
All  of     our  children     are  that  one.
```

Verse 6

```
          ‖C           |F           |C           |           |
There  is  a  vision  that  shines  in  the  darkness.

C                       |F           |C           |           |
That  one  vision  is  all  of  our  dreams.

F  C/F  F   |        C/F    F        |C           |        ‖
All  of     our  dreams     are  that  one.
```

Chorus 2

F   G |C |
It is a vision of heav - en.

F   G |C |
It is a child of prom - ise.

F   G |C |
It is a song of life.

F   G |C G C | G C
It is the river of no re-grets.

Outro

‖G   F |C
Let this be a voice for the mountains.

|G   F |C
Let this be a voice for the river.

|G   F |C
Let this be a voice for the forest.

|G   F |C
Let this be a voice for the flowers.

|G   F |C
Let this be a voice for the desert.

|G   F |C
Let this be a voice for the ocean.

|G   F |C
Let this be a voice for the children.

|G   F |C
Let this be a voice for the dreamers.

|G   F |C G C | G C   ‖
Let this be a voice of no re-grets, no re-grets.

Autograph

Words and Music by
John Denver

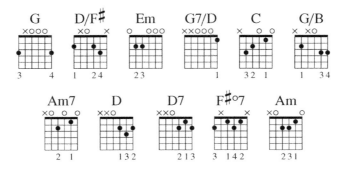

Verse 1

G   D/F# |Em   G7/D |
Here I am and closing my eyes   again,

C   G/B |Am7
Trying so hard   not to see

            D |G
All the things   that I see.

        D/F# |Em   G7/D
Almost willing to lie   again,

    |C   G/B |Am7
I swear that it just   isn't so,

    D |G
It just isn't me.

        D/F# |Em   G7/D
We are never a-lone

        |C   G/B Am7 G |D   D7 ‖
Even though we'd like to be.

Verse 2

G   **D/F♯** |Em   G7/D |
Then I go and open my eyes   again,

C   **G/B**   **|Am7**
Love in your eyes   is the thing

               D   **|G**
That I'd most like to see.

         D/F♯ |Em   G7/D
I'd be willing to die   again,

  |C   **G/B**   **|Am7**
To know of a place   and a time

           D   **|G**
Where it always could be,

         D/F♯ |Em   G7/D
To be always with you

   |C **G/B** **Am7** **G** **|D**   ‖
And you al - ways with me.

Chorus

F♯°**7**   **|G** |
This is my autograph

Am   **D7**   **|G** |
Here in the songs   that I sing,

F♯°**7**   **|G** |
Here in my cry and my laugh,

Am   **D7**   **|G**
Here in the love   that I bring,

         D/F♯ |Em   G7/D
To be always with you

   |C **G/B** **Am7** **G** **|D**   ‖
And you al - ways with me.

Verse 3

G   **D/F♯** |Em   G7/D |
Say a prayer and open your heart   again,

C   **G/B** |**Am7**
You are the love   and the light

            D |**G**
That we all need to see,

        D/F♯ |Em   G7/D |
Always willing to shine   and then

C   **G/B** |**Am7**
Peace on this earth   is the way

           D |**G**
That it always can be,

        D/F♯ |Em   G7/D
To be always with you

     |**C**   **G/B Am7 G** |**D** ||
And you al - ways with me.

Repeat Chorus

The Eagle and the Hawk

Words by John Denver
Music by John Denver and Mike Taylor

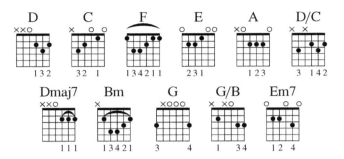

Verse

D
I am the eagle, I live in high country,

|**D** | |**C** |
In rocky cathedrals that reach to the sky.

D |
I am the hawk and there's blood on my feathers,

|**D** | |**C**
But time is still turning, they soon will be dry.

|**D** | |
And all those who see me and all who believe in me

D | |**F** |**E** |**A** | | |
Share in the freedom I feel when I fly.

Outro

||**D** |**D/C** **A** |
Come dance with the west wind and touch on the mountaintops,

Dmaj7 **Bm** |**G** **A**
Sail o'er the canyons and up to the stars,

|**D** **D/C** |**G/B** **D**
And reach for the heavens and hope for the future,

|**D/C** **G/B** |**Em7** |**A** | ||
And all that we can be and not what we are.

Flying for Me

Words and Music by
John Denver

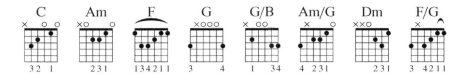

Verse 1

|**C**
Well, I guess that you probably know by now

|**Am**
I   was one who wanted to fly.

|**F** |**G** |**C** |**F**
I wanted to ride on that arrow of fire right up into heaven.

|**C**
And I wanted to go for ev-ery man,

|**Am**
Every child, every mother of chil-dren.

|**F** |**G** |**C** |**F**
I wanted to carry the dreams of all the people right up to the stars.

Verse 2

||**C**
And I prayed that I'd find that an-swer there,

|**Am**
Or maybe I would find the song

|**F** |**G** |**C** |**F**
Giving a voice to all of the hearts   that cannot be heard.

|**C**
And for all of the ones who live in fear

|**Am**
And all of those who stand apart,

|**F** |**G** |**C** |
My being there would bring us a little step closer togeth-er.

Chorus 1

‖**F**
They were flying for me,

|**G**　　　　　　　　|**C**
They were fly - ing for everyone.

　　　　　　　　　|**F**　　　　|**G**　　　　　　　　|**C**
They were trying to see　a brighter day for each and everyone.

　　　　　　|**F**
They gave us their light,

　　　　　|**G**　　　　　　　　　　|**Am**　　|**F**
They gave us their spirit and all they could be.

　　　G　　　|**C**　　|**F**
They were flying for me,

　　　G　　　|**C**　　|**F G** |**C G/B** |**Am Am/G**
They were flying for me.

Interlude

　　　‖**F**　　　　　　　　　　　|**G**
And I wanted to wish on the Milk-y Way

　　　　　|**C**　　　**G/B**　　　|**Am Am/G**
And dance　upon a falling star.

　　　　　　|**F**　　　　　|**Dm**　　　　|**F**　　　　　　　　|**F/G**　|**G**　　　|
I wanted to give myself and free myself, en-join myself with it all!

C　　|　　|**Am**　　|　　|**F**　|**G**　|**C**　|**F**

　　　|**C**　　　　　　　　　|
Given the chance to dream, it can be done,

|**Am**　　　　　　　　　|
The promise of tomorrow is real.

　　|**F**　　　　　　　|**G**　　　　　　|**C**　　|
Children of spaceship Earth, the future belongs to us all.

Chorus 2

‖F
She was flying for me,

|G |C
She was fly - ing for everyone.

       |F |G |C
She was trying to see a brighter day for each and everyone.

    |F
She gave us her light,

     |G |Am |F
She gave us her spirit and all she could be.

    G |C
She was flying for me.

Outro-Chorus

‖F
They were flying for me,

    |G |C
They were fly - ing for everyone.

       |F |G |C
They were trying to see a brighter day for each and everyone.

    |F
They gave us their light,

     |G |Am |F
They gave us their spirit and all they could be.

   G |C |F
They were flying for me,

   G |C |F
They were flying for me,

   G |C |F
They were flying for me,

   G |C |F G |C ‖
They were flying for me.

I Want to Live

Words and Music by
John Denver

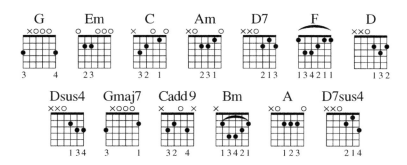

Verse 1

|G |Em
There are children raised in sorrow on a scorched and barren plain.

|C   Am |G   D7
There are children raised be-neath the golden sun.

|G |Em
There are children of the water, children of the sand,

|C   Am |F |D   Dsus4
And they cry out through the universe, their voices raised as one.

Chorus 1

D |G   Gmaj7
I want to live, I want to grow,

|C   Cadd9
I want to see, I want to know,

|Bm   C
I want to share what I can give.

|D   G | | D7
I want to be, I want to live.

Verse 2

‖G |Em
Have you gazed out on the ocean, seen the breaching of a whale?

|C   Am |G   D7
Have you watched the dolphins frolic in the foam?

|G |Em
Have you heard the song the humpback hears five hundred miles away

|C   Am |F |D   Dsus4
Telling tales of ancient history of passages and home?

Chorus 2

D |G   **Gmaj7**
I want to live, I want to grow,

|**C**   **Cadd9**
I want to see, I want to know,

|**Bm**   **C**
I want to share what I can give.

|**D**   **G** |
I want to be, I want to live.

Interlude

‖**Am** |**Em**
For the worker and the warrior, the lover and the liar,

|**F**   **Am** |**G**
For the native and the wan - derer in kind,

|**Am** |**Em**
For the maker and the user and the mother and her son,

|**F**   **Am** |**F** |**D7**
I am looking for my family and all of you are mine.

Verse 3

‖**G** |**Em**
We are standing all together face to face and arm in arm.

|**C**   **Am** |**G** **D7**
We are standing on the threshhold of a dream.

|**G** |**Em**
No more hunger, no more killing, no more wasting life away.

|**C**   **Am** |**F** |**D** **Dsus4**
It is simply an i-dea and I know its time has come.

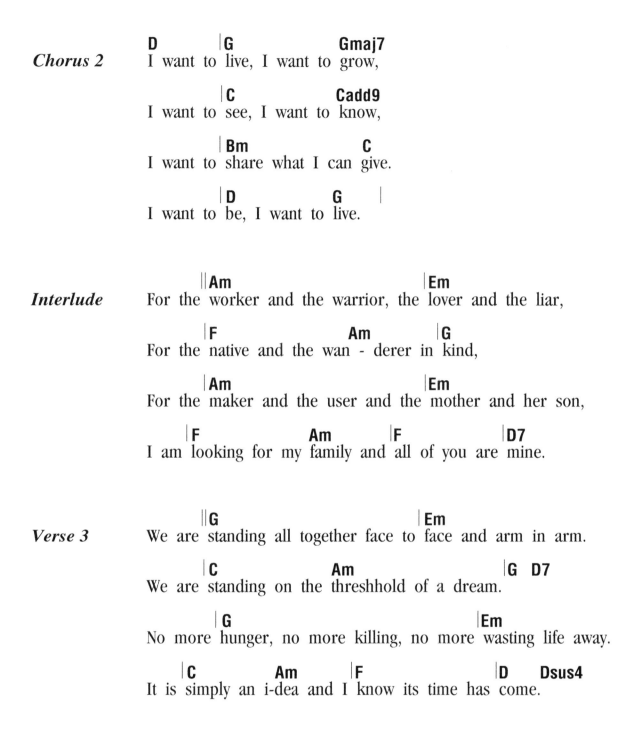

Outro-Chorus

D   ‖G   Gmaj7
I want to live, I want to grow,

      |C   Cadd9
I want to see, I want to know,

      |Bm   A
I want to share what I can give.

      |D7
I want to be...

      |G   Gmaj7
I want to live, I want to grow,

      |C   Cadd9
I want to see, I want to know,

      |Bm   A
I want to share what I can give.

      |D7 |G   Gmaj7 |C   Cadd9 |Bm   A |D7
I want to be, I want to live.

      |G   Gmaj7
I want to live, I want to grow,

      |C   Cadd9
I want to see, I want to know,

      |Bm   A
I want to share what I can give.

      |D7 |Gmaj7 |Cmaj9
I want to be, I want to live,

      |D7sus4   D7 |G   ‖
I want to live,   I want to live!

Let Us Begin
(What Are We Making Weapons For?)

Words and Music by
John Denver

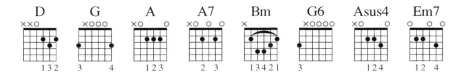

Verse 1

D
I am the son of a grassland farmer,

D   **G**
Western Oklahoma, nineteen forty-three.

|G   **|D |A**
I always felt grateful to live in the land of the free.

|D
I gave up my father to South Korea,

  |D   **|G |**
The mind of my brother to Vietnam.

G   **|D |A7**
Now there's a banker who says I must give up my land.

  |D
There are four generations of blood in this topsoil,

D   **|G**
Four generations of love on this farm.

|G   **|D | ||**
Be-fore I give up I would gladly give up my right arm.

Chorus

A7 | D |
What are we making weapons for?

Bm   G |A7   D
Why keep on feed - ing the war   machine?

    |A7 | D |
We take it right out of the mouths of our ba - bies,

A7 | D
Take it away from the hands of the poor.

     |G   D   A |D | | | ||
Tell me, what are we making weapons for?

Verse 2

D |
I had a son and my son was a soldier.

    |D | |G
He was so like my father, he was so much like me.

    |G | |D | A
To be a good comrade was the best that he dreamed he could be.

    |D |
He gave up his future to revolution,

    |D | |G
His life to a battle that just can't be won,

    |G | |D |A7
For this is not living, to live at the point of a gun.

    |D |
I remem - ber the nine hundred days of Leningrad,

    |D | |G
The sound of the dying, the cut of the cold,

    |G | |D | ||
I re-member the moments I prayed I would never grow old.

Repeat Chorus

Verse 3

‖**D** |
For the first time in my life I feel like a prisoner,

|**D** | **G**
A slave to the ways of the powers that be,

   |**G** | |**D** |**A7**
And I fear for my children as I fear for the future I see.

              |**D** | |
Tell me, how can it be we're still fighting each other?

D | |**G**
What does it take for a people to learn?

   |**G** | |**D** | ‖
If our song is not sung as a chorus, we surely will burn.

Repeat Chorus

Outro
            A   **D** ‖**G6** |**D** |
Have we for - got - ten

           |**D**   **A**   **D** |**G6** |**D** |
All the lives   that were giv - en,

           |**D**   **A**   **D** |**G6** |**D** |
All the vows   that were tak - en

          |**D** |**A** |**Asus4** |**A** |
Saying never a-gain?

G |**Em7** |**D** |
Now for the first time,

   |**D**   **A** **D** |**G6** |**D** |
This could be the last time.

  |**D**   **A** **D** |**G6** |**D** |**A** |
If peace is our vision,

A |**D** |
Let us be-gin.

Repeat Outro

Matthew

Words and Music by
John Denver

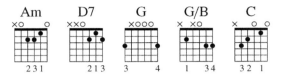

Intro-Verse

              | **|Am** | **|D7**
I had an un-cle, name of Matthew,

           |D7   **|G** | |
He was his father's only boy.

         |G   **|Am** | **|D7**
Born just south of Colby, Kansas,

          |D7   **|G**
He was his mother's pride and joy.

Chorus

         ‖G   **G/B** **|C**   **G/B** **|Am** | |
Yes, and joy was just a thing that he was raised on.

D7 | **|G** | |
Love was just a way to live and die.

G   **G/B** **|C**   **G/B** **|Am** | |
Gold was just a windy Kan - sas wheat field.

D7 | **|G** | |
Blue was just the Kan-sas summer sky.

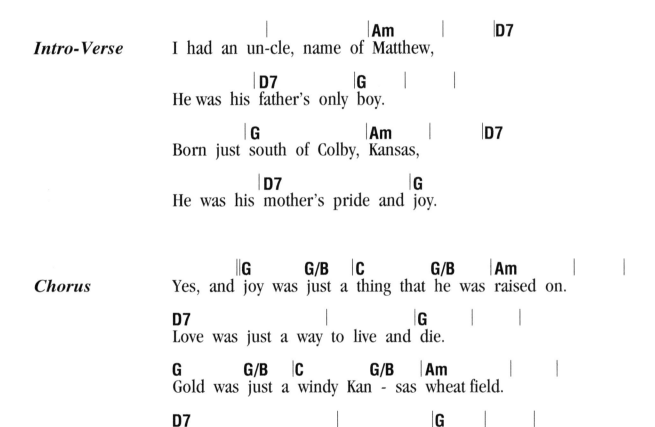

Verse 1

        |G ||Am | |D7
All the sto - ries that he told me

        |D7 |G | |
Back when I was just a lad.

        |G |Am | |D7
All the memories that he gave me,

        |D7 |G | |
All the good times that he had.

        |G |Am | |D7
Growin' up a Kansas farm boy

        |D7 |G | |
Life is mostly havin' fun,

        |G |Am | |D7
Ridin' on his daddy's shoulders

        |D7 |G
Behind a mule beneath the sun.

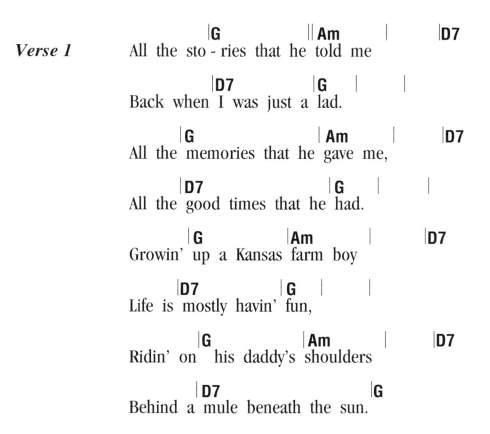

Repeat Chorus

Verse 2

        |G ||Am | |D7
Well, I guess there were some hard times

        |D7 |G | |
And I'm told some years were lean.

        |G |Am | |D7
They had a storm in 'forty-seven,

        |D7 |G | |
A twister came and stripped 'em clean.

        |G |Am | |D7
He lost the farm and lost his family,

        |D7 |G | |
He lost the wheat and lost his home,

        |G |Am | |D7
But he found the family bible,

        |D7 |G
A faith as solid as a stone.

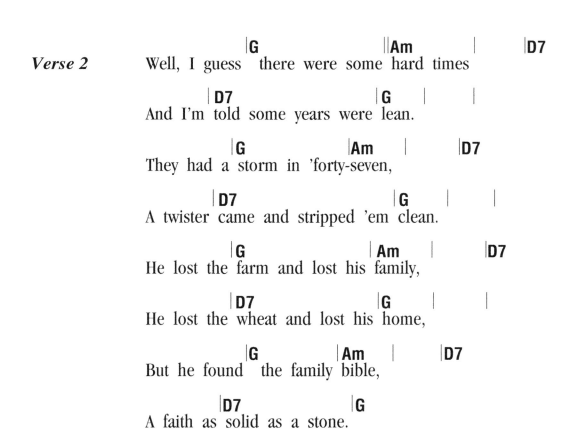

Repeat Chorus

Verse 3

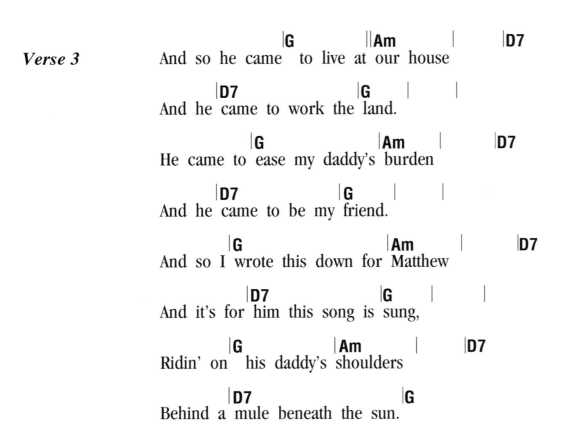

```
            |G          ||Am        |      |D7
And  so  he  came   to  live  at  our  house

      |D7                  |G        |      |
And  he  came  to  work  the  land.

            |G              |Am       |      |D7
He  came  to  ease  my  daddy's  burden

      |D7              |G        |      |
And  he  came  to  be  my  friend.

      |G                  |Am        |      |D7
And  so  I  wrote  this  down  for  Matthew

      |D7              |G        |      |
And  it's  for  him  this  song  is  sung,

      |G            |Am        |      |D7
Ridin'  on   his  daddy's  shoulders

      |D7                      |G
Behind  a  mule  beneath  the  sun.
```

Repeat Chorus (2X)

Raven's Child

Words by Joe Henry and John Denver
Music by John Denver

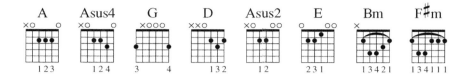

Verse 1

A |**Asus4** |
Raven's child is chas - ing salvation,

A |**Asus4** |**A** |**Asus4**
Black beak turned white from the crack and the snow.

      |**A** |**Asus4**
On the streets of despair the answer is simple,

 |**A**   **G** |**D** |**A**   **Asus4**| **A**
A spoonful of mercy can set free the soul.

      |**D** |
The drug king sits on his arrogant throne,

 |**D** |**A**   **Asus2**| **A** |
A-way and above and a-part.

D | |
Even children are twisted to serve him,

E | |**A**   **Asus4**| |**A** **Asus4**| ||
Greed has corrupted what once was a heart.

Verse 2

A |**Asus4** |
Raven's child keeps vig   -   il for freedom,

A |**Asus4** |**A** |**Asus4**
Trades for the arms that once made her strong.

 |**A** |**Asus4** |
With nuclear warheads and lasers in heaven,

A   **G** |**D** |**A**   **Asus4**| **A**
Fear does the choosing be-tween right and wrong.

 |**D**
The arms king sits on his arrogant throne,

 |**D** |**A**   **Asus2**| **A** |
A-way and above and a-part.

D
Bankers assure him he needn't care,

E | |**A**   **Asus4**| |**A** **Asus4**| ||
Greed makes a stone of what once was a heart.

Verse 3

A |**Asus4** |
Raven's child is wash -   ing the water,

A |**Asus4** |**A** |**Asus4** |
All her wing feathers blackened with tar.

A |**Asus4**
Prince William shoreline, an unwanted highway

 |**A**   **G** |**D** |**A**   **Asus4**| **A**
Of asphalt and anger, an elegant scar.

 |**D**
The oil king sits on his arrogant throne,

 |**D** |**A**   **Asus2**| **A** |
A-way and above and a-part.

D
Lawyers have warned him he mustn't speak,

 |**E** | |**A**   **Asus4**| **A** ||
And greed has made silent what once was a heart.

Interlude

```
Bm                              |E
Still there are walls that come tumbling down

      |A                      |F♯m     |
For people who yearn to be free.

Bm                             |A
Still there are hearts that long to be opened

      |D                  |E        |       ||
And eyes that are longing to see.
```

Verse 4

```
A                      |Asus4              |
Raven's child is our constant companion,

A                      |Asus4        |A      |Asus4     |
Sticks like a shadow to all    that is done.

A                      |Asus4
Try as we may we just   can't escape him,

   |A           G         |D          |A       Asus4| A
The source of our sorrow and shame. We are one.

      |D                      |
The true King sits on a heavenly throne,

         |D                  |A      Asus2| A
Never a-way nor above nor a-part.

      |D                      |
With wisdom and mercy and constant compassion,

   |E                |        |A      Asus4|      |A   Asus4|        ||
He lives in the love that lives in our hearts.
```

Outro

```
A                      |Asus4              |A   Asus4|       |
Raven's child is wash   -    ing the water.

A                      |Asus4        |A   Asus4|       |
Raven's child keeps vigil  for freedom.

A                      |Asus4        |A   Asus4|       |
Raven's child, chas   -   ing salvation.

A                      |Asus4              |A   Asus4|   |A      ||
Raven's child is our constant companion.
```

Rocky Mountain High

Words and Music by
John Denver and Mike Taylor

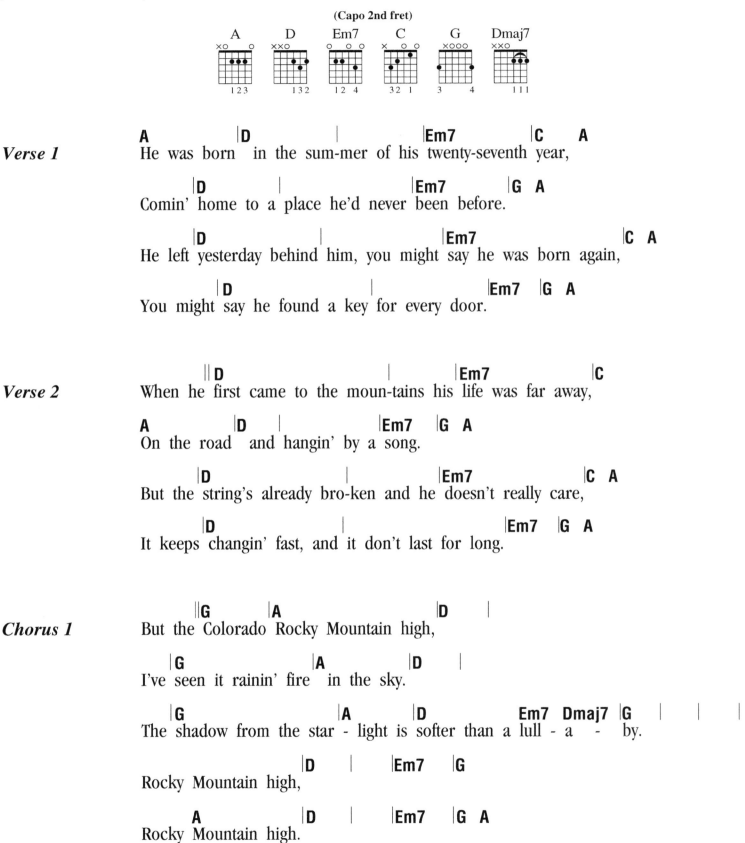

(Capo 2nd fret)

A   D   Em7   C   G   Dmaj7

Verse 1

|A |D | |Em7 |C   A
He was born in the sum-mer of his twenty-seventh year,

|D | |Em7 |G A
Comin' home to a place he'd never been before.

|D | |Em7 |C A
He left yesterday behind him, you might say he was born again,

|D | |Em7 |G A
You might say he found a key for every door.

Verse 2

||D | |Em7 |C
When he first came to the moun-tains his life was far away,

A |D | |Em7 |G A
On the road and hangin' by a song.

|D | |Em7 |C A
But the string's already bro-ken and he doesn't really care,

|D | |Em7 |G A
It keeps changin' fast, and it don't last for long.

Chorus 1

||G |A |D |
But the Colorado Rocky Mountain high,

|G |A |D |
I've seen it rainin' fire in the sky.

|G |A |D   Em7 Dmaj7 |G | |
The shadow from the star - light is softer than a lull - a - by.

|D | |Em7 |G
Rocky Mountain high,

A |D | |Em7 |G A
Rocky Mountain high.

Verse 3

    ‖**D** | |**Em7** |**C** **A**

He climbed   Cathedral Moun-tains, he saw silver clouds below,

    |**D** | |**Em7** |**G** **A**

He saw everything as far as you can see.

      |**D** | |**Em7** |**C** **A**

And they say that he got cra-zy once and he tried to touch the sun,

    |**D** | |**Em7** |**G** **A**

And he lost a friend but kept his memory.

Verse 4

    ‖**D** | |**Em7** |**C**

Now he walks in quiet sol-itude the forests and the streams,

A |**D** | |**Em7** |**G** **A**

Seeking grace in every step he takes.

    |**D** | |**Em7** |**C** **A**

His sight has turned inside himself to try and understand

    |**D** | |**Em7** |**G** **A**

The se-renity of a clear blue mountain lake.

Chorus 2

    ‖**G**   **A** |**A** |**D** |

And the Colorado Rocky Mountain high,

  |**G** |**A** |**D** | |**G**

I've seen it rainin' fire in the sky.

      |**A** |**D** **Em7** **Dmaj7** |**G** | |

Talk to God and listen to the cas-ual   re - ply.

      |**D** | |**Em7** |**G**

Rocky Mountain high,

   A |**D** | |**Em7** |**G** **A**

Rocky Mountain high.

Verse 5

||D | |Em7 |C A

Now his life is full of won-der but his heart still knows some fear

|D | |Em7 |G A

Of a simple thing he cannot compre-hend:

|D | |Em7 |C A

Why they try to tear the moun-tains down to bring in a couple more

|D | |Em7 |G A

More people, more scars upon the land.

Chorus 3

||G |A   D |

And the Colorado Rocky Mountain high,

|G |A |D |

I've seen it rainin' fire in the sky.

|G |A |D   Em7 Dmaj7 |G | | |

I know he'd be a poor - er man if he never saw an ea - gle   fly.

|D | |Em7 |G

Rocky Mountain high,

A |D |

Rocky Mountain high.

Outro-Chorus

||G |A |D |

It's a Colorado Rock - y Mountain high,

|G |A |D | |

I've seen it rainin' fire in the sky.

G |A |D   Em7 D |G | | |

Friends around the camp - fire and everybod - y's high.

|D | |Em7 |G

Rocky Mountain high,

A |D | |Em7 |G

Rocky Mountain high,

A |D | |Em7 |G

Rocky Mountain high,

A |D | ||

Rocky Mountain high.

Shanghai Breezes

Words and Music by
John Denver

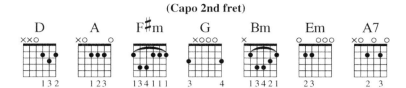

(Capo 2nd fret)

Verse 1

|D   A |F#m   G
It's funny how you sound as if you're right next door

      |D   Bm |Em A7
When you're really half a world away.

|D   A |F#m   G
I just can't seem to find the words I'm looking for,

|D   Bm |Em A7
To say the things that I want to say.

Verse 2

‖D   A |F#m   G
I can't remember when I felt so close to you,

   |D   Bm |Em A7 |
It's almost more than I can bear.

D   A |F#m   G
Though I seem a half a million miles from you,

      |D   Bm |Em A7
You are in my heart and living there.

Chorus 1

‖D   G |D   Bm
And the moon and the stars are the same ones you see,

   |Em   A7 |D A7
It's the same old sun up in the sky.

      |D   G |D   Bm
And your voice in my ear is like heav - en to me,

   |Em   A7 |D |Em F#m |G A7
Like the breezes here in old Shanghai.

Verse 3

    ‖**D**   **A** |**F♯m**   **G**
There are lovers who walk hand in hand in the park

    |**D**   **Bm** |**Em A7**
And lovers who walk all alone.

     |**D**   **A** |**F♯m**   **G**
There are lovers who lie unafraid in the dark

    |**D**   **Bm** |**Em** **A7**
And lovers who long for home.

Verse 4

    ‖**D**   **A** |**F♯m**   **G**
I couldn't leave you even if I wanted to,

     |**D**   **Bm** |**Em A7**
You're in my dreams and always near.

     |**D**   **A** |**F♯m**   **G**
And es-pecially when I sing the songs I wrote for you,

     |**D**   **Bm** |**Em A7**
You are in my heart and living there.

Chorus 2

     ‖**D**   **G** |**D**   **Bm**
And the moon and the stars are the same ones you see,

     |**Em**   **A7** |**D A7**
It's the same old sun up in the sky.

     |**D**   **G** |**D**   **Bm**
And your face in my dreams is like heav - en to me,

     |**Em**   **A7** |**D** ‖
Like the breezes here in old Shanghai.

Interlude

```
Em                    |F♯m           Bm   |
Shanghai breezes, cool and clear-ing,

G            A7        |D      |
Evening's sweet   caress.

Em                    |F♯m         D
Shanghai breezes, soft and gen - tle,

 |G          Em          |          A7
Re-mind me of     your ten-derness.
```

Chorus 3

```
        ‖D          G              |D            Bm
And the moon and the stars are the same   ones you see,

    |Em           A7          |D A7
It's the same old sun up  in the sky.

        |D          G              |D            Bm
And your love in my life is like heav - en to me,

    | Em          A7           |D A7
Like the breezes here in old Shanghai.
```

Outro-Chorus

```
        ‖D          G              |D            Bm
And the moon and the stars are the same   ones you see,

    |Em           A7          |D A7
It's the same old sun up  in the sky.

        |D          G              |D            Bm
And your love in my life is like heav - en to me,

    | Em          A7           |D
Like the breezes here in old Shanghai.

        | Em          A7        |D        ‖
Just like the breezes here in old Shang-hai.
```

To the Wild Country

Words and Music by
John Denver

(Capo 2nd fret)

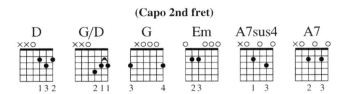

Verse 1

|D |G/D D
There are times   I fear I lose myself,

|G   Em |D
I don't know who   I am,

|G   Em |D   G |A7sus4 |A7
I get caught up in   the strug - gle and the strain.

|D |G/D D
With my back against a stone   wall,

|G |D
My finger in the dam,

|G   Em |D   G |A7sus4 |A7
I'm losin' strength   and goin' down again.

Verse 2

‖D |G/D D
When I take a look around   me,

|G |D
My eyes can't find the sun,

|G   Em |D   G |A7sus4 |A7
There's nothin' wild   as far as I can see.

|D |G/D D
Then my heart turns to Alas - ka

|G |D |
And freedom on the run,

G   Em |D   G |A7sus4 |A7
I can hear   her spirit calling me.

Chorus 1

```
    G     ‖Em  D  |G Em           |D
To the moun-tains,   I  can rest   there.

    G     |Em  D  |G Em           |A7
To the riv - ers,    I   will be strong.

    G     |Em  D  |G Em           |D
To the for - ests,     I'll find peace there.

    G     |Em  D  |G Em |A7          |D          |G/D  D
To the wild coun-try,        where I be-long.
```

Verse 3

```
                ‖D             |G/D  D
Oh, I know   sometimes I wor-ry

     |G           Em           |D
On worldly ways     and means.

      |G        Em      |D     G      |A7sus4    |A7
And I can see    the fu - ture killing me

       |D             |G/D  D
On a misbegotten high  -  way

    |G                        |D
Of prophesies  and dreams,

    |G         Em      |D     G    |A7sus4    |A7
A road to no - where and e-ternity.
```

Verse 4

‖**D** |**G/D D**
And I know it's just chang - es

 |**G** |**D** |
And mankind marchin' on,

G   **Em** |**D**   **G** |**A7sus4** |**A7**
I know we can't live in yesterday.

  |**D** |**G/D**   **D**
But com-pared to what we're los - in'

 |**G** |**D**
And what it means to me,

 |**G**   **Em** |**D**   **G** |**A7sus4** |**A7**
I'd give my life   and throw the rest a-way.

Chorus 2

G   ‖**Em**   **D** |**G Em** |**D**
To the moun-tains,   I   can rest   there.

G |**Em D** |**G Em** |**A7**
To the riv - ers,   I   will be strong.

G |**Em D** |**G Em** |**D**
To the for - ests,   I'll find peace there.

G |**Em D** |**G Em** |**A7** |**D**
To the wild coun-try,   I be-long.

G |**Em D** |**G Em** |**A7** |**D** |**G/D D** |**G Em** |**D**   ‖
To the wild coun-try,   where I be-long.

Wild Montana Skies

Words and Music by
John Denver

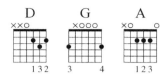

Verse 1

         |D | |G |D |
He was born in the Bitterroot Valley in the early mornin' rain,

 D | | |A
Wild geese over the wa-ter headin' north and home again,

         |D | |G |D
Bringin' a warm   wind from the south, bringin' the first   taste of the spring,

     |D | |A |D |
His mother took him to her breast and softly she did sing:

Chorus 1

      ‖G |A |D |
Oh, oh, Mon-tana, give this child a home,

        |G |A |D |
Give him the love   of a good family and a woman of his own,

        |G |A |D |G
Give him a fire in his heart, give him a light   in his eyes,

           |D | |A |D | |G A D
Give him the wild   wind for a broth-er and the wild Montana skies.

Verse 2

      ‖D | |G |D
His mother died that summer, he never learned to cry.

      |D | | |A
He never knew his fa-ther, he never did ask why.

      |D | |G |D
And he never knew the an-swers that would make an easy way,

      |D | |A |D |
But he learned to know the wil-derness and to be a man that way.

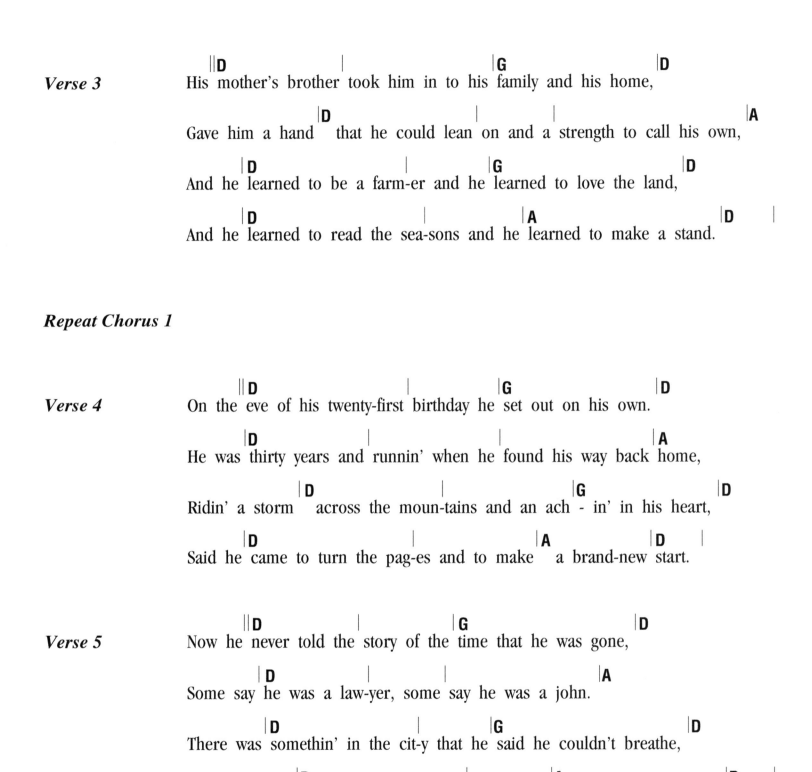

Verse 3

‖**D** | |**G** |**D**
His mother's brother took him in to his family and his home,

|**D** | | |**A**
Gave him a hand that he could lean on and a strength to call his own,

|**D** | |**G** |**D**
And he learned to be a farm-er and he learned to love the land,

|**D** | |**A** |**D** |
And he learned to read the sea-sons and he learned to make a stand.

Repeat Chorus 1

Verse 4

‖**D** | |**G** |**D**
On the eve of his twenty-first birthday he set out on his own.

|**D** | | |**A**
He was thirty years and runnin' when he found his way back home,

|**D** | |**G** |**D**
Ridin' a storm across the moun-tains and an ach - in' in his heart,

|**D** | |**A** |**D** |
Said he came to turn the pag-es and to make a brand-new start.

Verse 5

‖**D** | |**G** |**D**
Now he never told the story of the time that he was gone,

|**D** | | |**A**
Some say he was a law-yer, some say he was a john.

|**D** | |**G** |**D**
There was somethin' in the cit-y that he said he couldn't breathe,

|**D** | |**A** |**D** |
And there was somethin' in the coun-try that he said he couldn't leave.

Repeat Chorus 1

Verse 6

‖D | G D
Now some say he was crazy, some are glad he's gone,

|D | | A
But some of us will miss him and we'll try to carry on,

|D | G D
Giving a voice   to the for-est, giving a voice   to the dawn,

|D | A D |
Giving a voice   to the wil-derness and the land that he lived on.

Chorus 2

‖G A D |
Oh, oh, Mon-tana, give this child a home,

|G A D |
Give him the love   of a good family and a woman of his own,

|G A D G
Give him a fire   in his heart, give him a light   in his eyes,

|D | A | D |
Give him the wild   wind for a broth-er and the wild Montana skies.

Outro-Chorus

‖G A D |
Oh, oh, Mon-tana, give this child a home,

|G A D |
Give him the love   of a good family and a woman of his own,

|G A D G
Give him a fire   in his heart, give him a light   in his eyes,

|D | |
Give him the wild   wind for a broth-er and the

A | | | D | G A D ‖
Wild   Montana skies.

The Strum & Sing series for guitar and ukulele provides an unplugged and pared-down approach to your favorite songs – just the chords and the lyrics, with nothing fancy. These easy-to-play arrangements are designed for both aspiring and professional musicians.

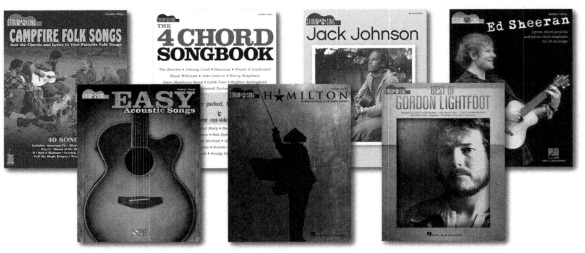

GUITAR

Acoustic Classics
00191891 ....$16.99

Adele
00159855 ....$12.99

Sara Bareilles
00102354 ....$12.99

The Beatles
00172234 ....$17.99

Blues
00159335 ....$12.99

Zac Brown Band
02501620 ....$19.99

Colbie Caillat
02501725 ....$14.99

Campfire Folk Songs
02500686 ....$15.99

Chart Hits of 2014-2015
00142554 ....$12.99

Chart Hits of 2015-2016
00156248 ....$12.99

Best of Kenny Chesney
00142457 ....$14.99

Christmas Carols
00348351 ....$14.99

Christmas Songs
00171332 ....$14.99

Kelly Clarkson
00146384 ....$14.99

Leonard Cohen
00265489 ....$16.99

Dear Evan Hansen
00295108 ....$16.99

John Denver Collection
02500632 ....$17.99

Disney
00233900 ....$17.99

Eagles
00157994 ....$14.99

Easy Acoustic Songs
00125478 ....$19.99

Billie Eilish
00363094 ....$14.99

The Five-Chord Songbook
02501718 ....$14.99

Folk Rock Favorites
02501669 ....$16.99

Folk Songs
02501482 ....$15.99

The Four-Chord Country Songbook
00114936 ....$16.99

The Four Chord Songbook
02501533 ....$14.99

Four Chord Songs
00249581 ....$16.99

The Greatest Showman
00278383 ....$14.99

Hamilton
00217116 ....$15.99

Jack Johnson
02500858 ....$19.99

Robert Johnson
00191890 ....$12.99

Carole King
00115243 ....$10.99

Best of Gordon Lightfoot
00139393 ....$15.99

John Mayer
02501636 ....$19.99

The Most Requested Songs
02501748 ....$19.99

Jason Mraz
02501452 ....$14.99

**Tom Petty –
Wildflowers & All the Rest**
00362682 ....$14.99

Elvis Presley
00198890 ....$12.99

Queen
00218578 ....$12.99

Rock Around the Clock
00103625 ....$12.99

Rock Ballads
02500872 ....$12.99

Rocketman
00300469 ....$17.99

Ed Sheeran
00152016 ....$14.99

The Six-Chord Songbook
02502277 ....$17.99

Chris Stapleton
00362625 ....$19.99

Cat Stevens
00116827 ....$17.99

Taylor Swift
01191699 ....$19.99

The Three-Chord Songbook
00211634 ....$14.99

Top Christian Hits
00156331 ....$12.99

Top Hits of 2016
00194288 ....$12.99

The Who
00103667 ....$12.99

Yesterday
00301629 ....$14.99

Neil Young – Greatest Hits
00138270 ....$16.99

UKULELE

The Beatles
00233899 ....$16.99

Colbie Caillat
02501731 ....$10.99

Coffeehouse Songs
00138238 ....$14.99

John Denver
02501694 ....$17.99

The 4-Chord Ukulele Songbook
00114331 ....$16.99

Jack Johnson
02501702 ....$19.99

John Mayer
02501706 ....$10.99

The Most Requested Songs
02501453 ....$15.99

Pop Songs for Kids
00284415 ....$17.99

Sing-Along Songs
02501710 ....$17.99

HAL•LEONARD®

halleonard.com
Visit our website to see full song lists
or order from your favorite retailer.

*Prices, contents and availability
subject to change without notice.*

Presenting the Best in
BLUEGRASS

THE REAL BLUEGRASS BOOK

Ballad of Jed Clampett • Bill Cheatham • Down to the River to Pray • Foggy Mountain Top • I'm Goin' Back to Old Kentucky • John Henry • Old Train • Pretty Polly • Rocky Top • Sally Goodin • Wildwood Flower • and more.
00310910 C Instruments...............................$39.99

BLUEGRASS

Guitar Play-Along
Book/CD Pack
8 songs: Duelin' Banjos • Foggy Mountain Breakdown • Gold Rush • I Am a Man of Constant Sorrow • Nine Pound Hammer • Orange Blossom Special • Rocky Top • Wildwood Flower.
00699910 Guitar...$17.99

BLUEGRASS GUITAR

by Happy Traum
Book/CD Pack
This guitar workbook covers every aspect of bluegrass playing, from simple accompaniment to advanced instrumentals.
14004656 Guitar...$27.99

BLUEGRASS GUITAR CLASSICS

22 Carter-style solos: Back Up and Push • The Big Rock Candy Mountain • Cotton Eyed Joe • Cumberland Gap • Down Yonder • Jesse James • John Henry • Little Sadie Long Journey Home • Man of Constant Sorrow • Midnight Special • Mule Skinner Blues • Red Wing • Uncle Joe • The Wabash Cannon Ball • Wildwood Flower • and more.
00699529 Solo Guitar..................................$8.99

BLUEGRASS GUITAR

Arranged and Performed by Wayne Henderson
Transcribed by David Ziegele
Book/CD Pack
10 classic bluegrass tunes: Black Mountain Rag • Fisher's Hornpipe • Leather Britches • Lime Rock • Sally Anne • Take Me Out to the Ball Game • Temperence Reel • Twinkle Little Star • and more.
00700184 Guitar Solo..................................$16.99

BLUEGRASS SONGS FOR EASY GUITAR

25 bluegrass standards: Alabama Jubilee • Arkansas Traveler • Bill Cheatham • Blackberry Blossom • The Fox • Great Speckled Bird • I Am a Pilgrim • New River Train • Red Rocking Chair • Red Wing • Sally Goodin • Soldier's Joy • Turkey in the Straw • and more.
00702394 Easy Guitar with Notes & Tab.......$15.99

www.halleonard.com

BLUEGRASS STANDARDS

by David Hamburger
16 bluegrass classics expertly arranged: Ballad of Jed Clampett • Blue Yodel No. 4 (California Blues) • Can't You Hear Me Calling • I'll Go Stepping Too • I'm Goin' Back to Old Kentucky • Let Me Love You One More Time • My Rose of Old Kentucky • We'll Meet Again Sweetheart • and more.
00699760 Solo Guitar..................................$7.99

FIRST 50 BLUEGRASS SOLOS YOU SHOULD PLAY ON GUITAR

arr. Fred Sokolow
Songs include: Arkansas Traveler • Cripple Creek • I Am a Man of Constant Sorrow • I'll Fly Away • Long Journey Home • Molly and Tenbrooks • Old Joe Clark • The Red Haired Boy • Rocky Top • Wabash Cannonball • Wayfaring Stranger • You Don't Know My Mind • and more!
00298574 Solo Guitar................................$15.99

FRETBOARD ROADMAPS – BLUEGRASS AND FOLK GUITAR

by Fred Sokolow
Book/CD Pack
This book/CD pack will have you playing lead and rhythm anywhere on the fretboard, in any key. You'll learn chord-based licks, moveable major and blues scales, major pentatonic "sliding scales," first-position major scales, and moveable-position major scales.
00695355 Guitar...$14.99

THE GUITAR PICKER'S FAKEBOOK

by David Brody
Compiled, edited and arranged by David Brody, this is the ultimate sourcebook for the traditional guitar player. It contains over 280 jigs, reels, rags, hornpipes and breakdowns from all the major traditional instrumental styles.
14013518 Melody/Lyrics/Chords.................$32.99

O BROTHER, WHERE ART THOU?

Songs include: Big Rock Candy Mountain (Harry McClintock) • You Are My Sunshine (Norman Blake) • Hard Time Killing Floor Blues (Chris Thomas King) • I Am a Man of Constant Sorrow (The Soggy Bottom Boys/Norman Blake) • Keep on the Sunny Side (The Whites) • I'll Fly Away (Alison Krauss and Gillian Welch) • and more.
00313182 Guitar...$22.99

HOT LICKS FOR BLUEGRASS GUITAR

by Orrin Star
Over 350 authentic bluegrass licks are included in this book, which also discusses how to apply the licks to create your own solos and expand your musical understanding and knowledge of the fingerboard.
14015430 Guitar Licks...............................$26.99

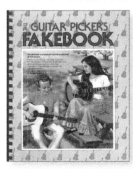

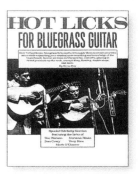